Library of
Davidson College

UGANDA
A Case Study
in African Political Development

UGANDA
A Case Study
in African Political Development

Peter M. Gukiina

UNIVERSITY OF NOTRE DAME PRESS
NOTRE DAME   LONDON

Copyright © 1972 by
University of Notre Dame Press
Notre Dame, Indiana 46556

Library of Congress Catalog
Card Number:72-3511

Printed in the United States of America
by NAPCO Graphic Arts,Inc.,New Berlin,
Wisconsin

To

My Mother, Mary Nambi

and to

My Brother, M. S. Bulago

Who have shared in the cost of the political changes of the sixties. May they live to see Uganda a united, democratic and prosperous nation.

Contents

Chapter-Opening Illustrations	ix
Preface	xi
Introduction	1
1 The Pre-Colonial Period	13
2 The Colonial Experience	41
3 National Consensus and the Struggle for National Unity	75
4 The Politics of Independence	95
5 The Post-Independence Politics and the Obote Revolution	110
6 Obote's Government and the Creation of National Consensus	141
Conclusion	164
Notes	176
Bibliography	187

Chapter-Opening Illustrations

Kigezi District *(by M. Nekam)*	1
Murchison Falls *(by Bro. Richard)*	13
Murchison National Park *(by A. Nekam)*	41
Karamajong and Their Spears *(by A. Nekam)*	75
Marketplace in West Nile District *(by A. Nekam)*	95
Outdoor Classroom *(by A. Nekam)*	110
Parliament *(by Bro. Richard)*	141
Karamajong Elder *(by M. Nekam)*	164

Preface

This historical and analytical examination of Uganda's political problems and development is a result of my positive response to my great desire to understand the political problems and aspirations of the peoples of Uganda to whom I am infinitely bound.

What has diverted and polluted the best energies of Uganda's traditional and modern leaderships and brought about drastic political changes, costly for all Ugandans, is the focus of this small volume.

This book relates past and recent political developments, social and economic changes in terms of humans responding to a new political situation in an environment of ethnic group traditions, values, customs and interests, mixed with the colonial sins still hovering over the African continent.

What this historical and analytical examination of Uganda's political environment aims to achieve is to put the political aspirations, successes and mistakes of the peoples of Uganda in a proper perspective. Hopefully a better understanding of African political problems and developments will also emerge.

I am indebted to the following professors at Kalamazoo College: Dr. Donald Flesche and Dr. Elton W. Ham of the Political Science Department, and to Professor William F. Pruitt of the History Department for reading the manuscript and offering valuable suggestions and criticism.

Introduction

I witnessed Uganda's struggle for independence, which was granted on October 9, 1962. On the basis of my own experience and knowledge of political events in my mother country Uganda, I can best characterize the struggle for independence as an era when all Ugandan politicians spoke highly of justice, freedom, liberty, equality, unity, brotherhood, and anti-authoritarianism. They were opposed to anything contrary to democratic principles.

Ugandan politicians were unanimously opposed to the use of the police and army as the main basis of implementing law and order. No politician that I can remember failed to reproach the colonial officers for their unnecessary use of force in denying the people some of their inalienable rights, namely freedom of association and expression.

Most Ugandans understood the rhetoric in terms of an inevitable downfall of British dictatorial and exploitive colonial rule and a return to some type of political system based predominantly on traditional forms of local government. In Buganda Kingdom, for instance, what was expected from independence was well articulated in the September, 1960, memorandum to Queen Elizabeth II submitted by members of the Lukiiko (parliament) of the Kingdom of Buganda.[1] The memorandum explained in detail the Baganda's constitutional plans for independence. A summary of the statement is an excellent outline for most of the significant goals Buganda sought from independence. As early as 1958, Buganda Kingdom had taken a firm stand in declaring that Buganda must have her own form of military alliance with Britain before independence. She also wanted to have her own police forces for the purpose of maintaining law and order.

In regard to the police forces, Buganda demanded that all present Ugandan police forces responsible for the Buganda Province should automatically come under the Buganda government's jurisdiction. Buganda also insisted that she have her own independent high court and district courts. The Buganda High Court was to be on an equal basis with the National High Court. Appeals from it would be to the East African Court of Appeal and finally the Privy Council. Commerce and industry located in Buganda were to be licensed in Buganda, and all excise duty was to go to the Buganda Kingdom Treasury. All existing institutions of learning in Buganda were to be under the jurisdiction of the Buganda government. Makerere University College was the only exception; Buganda would share in its administration but would allow it to continue to function as an East African inter-state institution. In short, Buganda intended to acquire a-l powers or most of the powers exercised by Her Majesty's representatives in Buganda.

The traditional leaders of the Baganda (people of Buganda Kingdom) had been negotiating for the above-mentioned powers since 1958. Failing to realize their demands through negotiations with the secretary of state of Her Majesty's government, the Buganda Lukiiko was in session from September 21 to 24, 1960, to consider a unilateral termination of British protection in Buganda. According to Apolo Nsibambi, a lecturer in political science at Makerere University College,

> Baganda felt that since Buganda as a whole was never conquered by the British and that since the British were freely invited by the Baganda to protect them, the Baganda retained their natural sovereignty and that they had the right to renounce British protection at any time and regain the responsibility of protecting the nation of Buganda.[2]

As a result of this feeling, in 1960 the Buganda Lukiiko passed a resolution on December 30, declaring in the name of God and the Nation of Buganda, that the British protection in Buganda was at an end as of midnight of December 31, 1960. I remember that all of the people in my village excitedly ran around the neighborhood shouting, "We are independent as of January 1, 1961."

However, the British persuaded and threatened Baganda out of their determination to be a separate autonomous state, with or without the approval of the colonial office. The abortive attempt of establishing a separate autonomous state of Buganda, made things absolutely clear. The overwhelming majority of the people of Buganda was wholeheartedly behind their Kabaka (King of Buganda) and the Kabaka's demands for an independent nation of Buganda, or at least for a near independent Buganda Kingdom operating within a loose federation with the other parts of Uganda.

Obviously, a very large majority of Baganda people expected and wanted independence to mean a return to a political system that would make their king the supreme head and law of Buganda. Attitudes and expectations like those in Buganda were also widely shared by other groups in Uganda, particularly by the kingdoms of Bunyoro, Ankole, Toro and Busoga. They all demanded federal status for their respective kingdoms, within independent Uganda, as a means of preserving their thrones and restoring power to their respective kings and other traditional leaders. Independence was widely and deeply regarded as a return of most political power to the traditional rulers.

To many Ugandans, the transfer of power from Her Majesty's government was not to be to an African central government, but to their respective local governments under the leadership of their traditional leaders.

Unlike the majority of Ugandans, most Westerners, as well as some of their Ugandan educated compatriots, took the rhetoric to mean a massive campaign for national independence and democracy--the type of democracy not far from what Adrian and Press called "the Frontier Precepts of Jacksonian Democracy."[3] Hundreds of well-educated Ugandans wanted and pushed ahead for a government by the common man. "One man one vote" was the topic of the day. They wanted a government for all Ugandans, not for a privileged class like the established traditional leaders and foreign economic interests. They stood firm by their demands that independence should be granted only after a general election in which all citizens over 21 years old would be qualified to vote freely for their own choice of candidates. Most Westerners and some Ugandans with formal education wanted independence to mean the establishment of an ideal democratic political system within the context of a British-type of parliamentary democracy.

Since independence, however, political events in Uganda have led to a development and consolidation of a political system remote from what was expected by most, if not all, Ugandans. By the end of 1966, President Obote's government (the national government of Uganda) had abolished the traditional forms of government and forced the traditional leaders out of Ugandan politics. The physical elimination of traditional leaders from politics marked the beginning of the consolidation of modernizing national leadership in the country. Since 1966, leaders committed to national unity and rapid economic growth have taken over all political powers at the expense of the traditional forms of leadership.

The consolidation has been one of the most remarkable political achievements of Uganda. But unfortunately, since 1966 this achievement has proved to be too costly in terms of human life, human suffering, human rights and democratic principles. Major revolutions and internal wars between the seventeenth and the nineteenth century in Great Britain, France, the United States, Germany and Italy led C. E. Black to the conclusion that:

> Traditional political systems normally do not make provision for fundamental reforms by constitutional means, and change in leadership that involves a displacement of the traditional oligarchy cannot be made without violence. Modern states may well be able to set their colonies on the road to independence without bloodshed . . . , but the transition from traditional to modern leadership has generally been violent.[4]

For Uganda the transfer of political power can be characterized as bloody, authoritarian, and revolutionary. The violent transfer of political power from the hands of tradition-bound leaders to Dr. Obote's nationalist regime did much more to shape the country's political system than any other issue in Ugandan politics. The transfer of power swiftly led Uganda from a loose federation to what some political scientists refer to as a "one man dictatorship."

Upon Dr. Obote's personal orders, the police burst into a cabinet meeting on February 22, 1966, and dragged five cabinet ministers to an unidentified destination for solitary confinement. The five ministers remained in detention, without trial, until the military coup on January 25, 1971. Immediately after their arrest Obote declared that he was temporarily assuming all governmental powers. Forty-eight hours later, Obote announced that the 1962 constitution had been suspended and the Uganda Parliament dissolved. He then declared that the offices of president and vice president no longer existed, thus ousting the Kabaka of Buganda from the office of president and Kyabazinga (King of Busoga) from the office of vice president.

With the Kabaka ungracefully ousted from the office of president, serious trouble was imminent in Buganda. The Buganda Lukiiko met in May to do exactly what the overwhelming majority of Baganda wanted. They responded to Obote's actions by passing a resolution ordering the central government personnel and property off Buganda soil by the end of May, 1966. Meanwhile, Obote responded and consolidated his power on May 22, by declaring a state of emergency for all of Uganda and soon afterwards by imposing his own constitution which swiftly transformed Uganda from a federal and semi-federal political system to a unitary state. The new constitution abolished all local governments and Dr.

Obote assumed the offices of prime minister, president and vice president respectively. Obote's constitution vested all executive powers in the executive president, eliminated the right of appeal to the Privy Council in London, and recognized the presence of traditional rulers in the kingdoms but forbade them to hold any public office. A new political era had begun: Obote was carefully maneuvering to stop all political activities in the country through military and police forces, and a potentially oppressive detention act was immediately put into action. The one man constitution remained in force from April, 1966, until September, 1967, when a new national constitution was adopted. In spite of the new constitution, the political atmosphere in Uganda remained far from democratic.

Since 1962 there have been no parliamentary elections. Elections were supposed to take place every five years. The five ex-ministers mentioned above were kept in prison, and Buganda remained under the state of emergency. Mr. Kiwanuka, a lawyer and president of the Democratic party--the only opposition party in Parliament--was later arrested and detained.

Abu Mayanja, a Ugandan lawyer and member of Parliament, expressed a general feeling in Uganda in his article published in *Transition*, stating that, "The government was still operating under outmoded colonial law . . . especially those laws designed by the colonial regime to suppress freedom of association and expression."[5] It is important to note that, immediately after the publication of Mayanja's article, Abu Mayanja and the editor of *Transition*, Mr. Meogy, were arrested and detained for publishing materials dangerous to what Obote's government called the peace and security of Uganda. In November, 1968, Chief Magistrate David Lubogo, a Ugandan, acquitted Mr. Mayanja and Mr. Meogy of the sedition charges brought against them, but both were rearrested as they were leaving the courtroom and detained under emergency regulations. Abu Mayanja's case is not an isolated example. On June 12, 1967, 22 persons were arrested for an alleged attempted coup against Obote's government. The trial opened July 2 and closed July 5 at the request of the public prosecutor. The court released the 22 persons on bond pending a new trial. But they were all rearrested as they left the courtroom.

Since independence, Uganda has also seen the creation of a government controlled Uganda Labor Congress and the abolition of the two old labor organizations--the Uganda Trade Union Congress and the Federation of Uganda Trade Unions.

The struggle for independence was a struggle for democratic principles, but what has happened in less than 10 years after independence is obviously far from a democratic political system. This study is an attempt to shed light on the main political and cultural forces which have brought about a political system very different from that desired and hoped for by the overwhelming majority of Ugandans. Those who viewed independence as a fortunate and welcome return to traditional authority are not only politically disappointed and frustrated but also reluctant to accept the idea that a just and desireable national government is possible. Those who consider independence in terms of Western concepts of democracy have been temporarily in a state of despair. There are, of course, many ways in which political observers and newspaper reporters can explain why democracy has so far failed to work in Uganda.

Some choose to understand Ugandan politics in terms of "tribalism" and regional hatred in Uganda. Others emphasize the corruption and power hunger of some Ugandan politicians. And to some diehard conservative Westerners with a colonial mentality, the explanation is simple and clear--Black people have no conceptions of freedom, and they lack the mental capacity and maturity to accept, appreciate and work for a democratic government. What the conservatives say about us seems to suggest that Black people look at freedom as dogs look at dollar bills. Most unfortunate is the attitude of some Ugandans, who freely but without proper perspective, choose to blame the whole situation on China and Russia. There are some Ugandans who strongly feel that it was a grave mistake for Uganda to enter into diplomatic relations with Russia and China. They view the Chinese and Russian embassies as the main latent forces in Uganda which have made democracy temporarily an unworkable political system for Uganda. Obote's prolonged tour of Eastern Europe and Red China in the summer of 1965, and his July 5-10 official visit to Yugoslavia in the same year, have been cited hundreds of times as evidence that Russia and China were behind his ruthless use of force to eradicate traditional rule in order to transform Uganda into a socialist authoritarian state.

The purpose of this study and analysis is not to claim that the so-called tribal and regional hatred or disrespect and mistrust have no place in Ugandan politics. Lack of political experience, real and imagined corruption of some politicans and the socialistic inclinations of Obote's government, all have some influence on political values and attitudes in Uganda. But a careful examination of political events in Uganda reveals that these aspects of Uganda's political environment are of minimal influence and they are not the most significant elements of Uganda's political environment.

This study has two main parts. Chapters 1-4 are detailed examinations of the presence or absence of a national concensus at the time of independence. Before one can understand and appreciate the political problems of Uganda, one must have a good idea of the traditional social and political systems that existed before and during the colonial era. Without this background, one cannot comprehend the values and attitudes within Uganda that have made temporary authoritarian rule not only necessary but inevitable. As one reads through Chapter 1, which deals with three varied peoples of Uganda and the concept of "tribalism," one must find it prudent to accept Ugandan politics in terms of ethnic group values, attitudes and myths. As a Ugandan and member of the Buganda ethnic group, I have consistently found it inadequate and extremely misleading to try to understand Ugandan politics in terms of a vague and often ill-conceived and confused concept of "tribalism."

The second part of this study examines in detail the successes and failures of Dr. Obote's attempts to create national consensus and peoples' confidence in himself and his government. Since the overthrow of traditional authority in 1966, Uganda's political system has been based on and maintained by military and police force. Meanwhile Dr. Obote and his government carried on an all-out campaign to legitimize his authority and to create support for a national political system. A careful examination of Dr. Obote's political maneuver and the circumstances in which he acted answer the crucial question of whether Obote's government would have succeeded or failed to generate a national political, social, and economic consciousness--the right kind of consciousness that would have made democratic government possible.

This study does not give clear-cut answers and solutions to Uganda's numerous political problems. It does, however, provide ample ground for one to know what to expect and what to praise or criticize when one decides to latently or actively participate or philosophize about the formative years of Ugandan politics.

1

The Pre-Colonial Period

Uganda, as we know it today, is an independent African state lying astride the equator on the central African plateau. The country is not much larger than Britain. It is 94,000 square miles, 16,836 of which are beautiful lakes and river valleys.[1] One-seventh of the total area is the open water of many lakes, including Lake Victoria. Often, Uganda is described as a land of rich, fertile valleys, towering snow-capped peaks, magnificent lakes and waterfalls, dense forests and vast plains teeming with wild game. Besides the natural beauty is the diversity of ethnic groups, each with its own individual culture, styles and traditions. The age-old traditions, institutions and ceremonies of each of Uganda's twenty-eight ethnic groups not only add to the fascinating color of the country but also continue to be very significant aspects of the unique political character of modern Uganda.

Uganda is a political creature of nineteenth century British imperialism and colonialism. A protectorate over Buganda Kingdom was formally and peacefully established in 1894 and was extended over most of the country two years later. Before effective British influence began in the 1890's, "Uganda" meant Buganda Kingdom, "Uganda" being the word for "Buganda" in Kiswahili.[2] Throughout the colonial period, the Buganda ethnic group alone covered one-fourth of the whole country.

Before colonization, the area was occupied by a diversity of ethnic groups, each with its own language, individual cultural, political and social styles and traditions. For at least two centuries most of these ethnic groups had existed as independent societies with their own kinds of political organizations. It is likely that 90 per cent of the people of each ethnic group had never spent a day outside their own groups--which means that to a great extent, each group had always existed economically, socially, politically and physically independent from all other groups. The political organizations, attitudes and values of these traditionally internally directed groups are the subject of this first chapter.

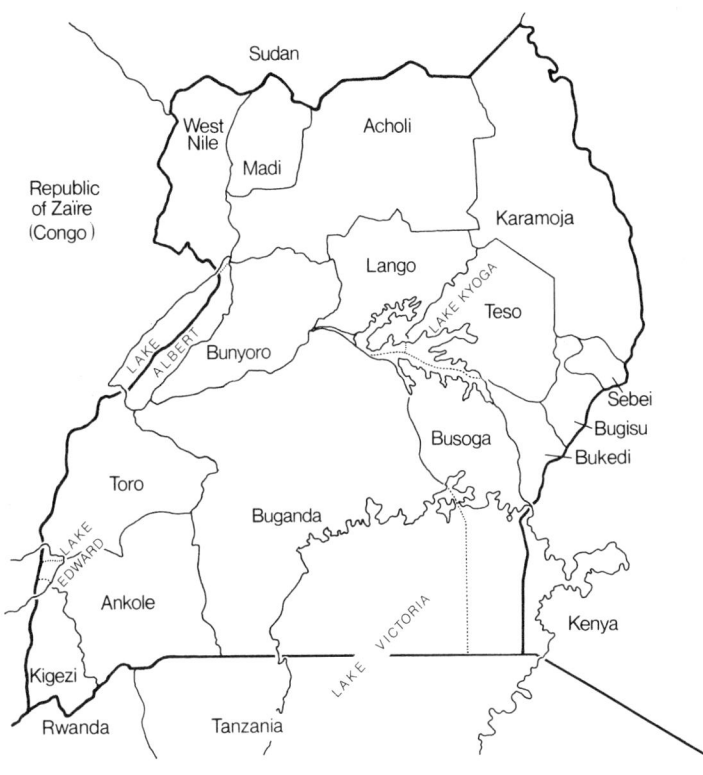

UGANDA

Before the different political ethos of some of these pre-colonial, politically independent societies can be objectively examined, it is necessary to deal with the concept of "tribalism" and its current usage. Such a consideration is necessary because most people today consciously and unconsciously tend to think in terms of "tribalism, tribal wars and centuries of tribal hatred" whenever one mentions the impact and significance of African traditional political and social values, attitudes, and/or systems on the current systems. In social sciences "tribe," or "tribalism" is not defined in neutral terms. If "tribe" were to be defined as a group that is a politically significant subdivision in a nation or a state and has some widespread consciousness of common, distinct identity and culture, it could be accepted. What appears, however, is that the "concept of tribalism" is always clothed in stereotypes and myths which some of the corrupt minds of nineteenth century imperialists and colonialists invented, exaggerated and sold to their people in order to justify and generate support for the colonial subjugation and economic exploitation of the African people.

Writing in 1902, J. A. Hobson, an English economist and correspondent for the *Manchester Guardian* from South Africa, pointed out that the colonization of tropical Africa was bad business for Great Britain but that it was very profitable for certain classes in Britain.[3] Like Mr. Hobson, many other British historians emphasized that by 1900, the smallest, least valuable and most uncertain British trade was done with the tropical possessions in

Africa. In terms of Great Britain as a whole, trade with Africa was considered irregular and dwindling.

Yet the colonization of Africa cannot be generally characterized as bad business. The funds spent in the colonies were expenditures of the mother country. But the immediate economic benefits of colonial policy and colonial situations were shared by certain groups of people in Britain. What this means is that even if colonial expenditures exceeded income, still the business of colonization remained and was expected to continue to be big profit business. As Mr. Hobson pointed out:

> Certain definite business and professional interests feeding upon imperialistic expenditures or upon the results of that expenditures, are found united in a strong, sympathy to support every imperialist exploit. . . . Here we have an important nucleus of Commercial Imperialism. Some of these trades, especially the shipbuilding, boilermaking, and gun and ammunition making trades, are conducted by large firms with immense capital whose heads are well aware of the use of political influence for trade purposes. These men are imperialistic by conviction; a pushful policy is good for them.[4]

It was these selfish money-grabbers who self-styled themselves as manufacturers and distributors of "civilization." They fed the British press all kinds of distorted stories about the African people in order to convince the British people that they had a God-given duty to free, civilize and elevate Africans--the "lower" races.

The worst products of British capitalism and imperialism of the nineteenth century were those who filled their mouths with noble phrases and expressions to give an appearance of a sincere, profound desire to establish good government, promote Christianity and eradicate slavery. They, at the same time, projected the African people, their traditions and institutions as the most primitive, most savage and most cruel and that this justifies their domination in order to extend civilization to the Dark Continent.

I am not going to claim that African societies were perfect. All societies have their good and bad points. What I want to point out here is that concepts of "tribe" and "tribalism" convey to most people a mixture of some aspects of African societies along with disparagements which were directly and indirectly a product of the worst kind of Western man's imagination.

According to Ronald Cohen, once one realizes that, contrary to what non-specialists think, a tribe is an immutable entity which is adaptive and which changes in relation to outside forces as well as to internal forces:

> It becomes nonsense to speak of "reverting" to tribalism or "ancient tribal rivalries." Instead, we must ask questions about the traditional ethnic identities in an area and the relationship of these to the traditional and modern political structures and then ask what has produced the contemporary ethnic identities and solidarities (or lack of them).[5]

Unfortunately, most Westerners and many Africans continue to interpret political events, particularly conflicts between different groups in an African state, in terms of "tribalism" and "tribal" hatred. But like Ronald Cohen, some social scientists have come to view the concepts of "tribalism" as misleading and difficult to understand. They therefore choose to use "ethnic society" instead of "tribe."

In order to have a clear and reliable understanding of Ugandan politics one must abandon the use of the terms "tribe," "tribalism" and "tribal hatred." These concepts or terms have been frequently used by colonial officials, former colonial officials, the Western press and, most unfortunately, by many African leaders in their search for power, money and prestige. These terms are an inexhaustible source of logical, but rarely correct, interpretations of political events in Africa.

In this regard, it is interesting to note Professor Burke's conversation with Dr. Edwardo Mondlane,[6] as described by Professor Burke in his speech at Duke University's Commonwealth Studies Center on February 15, 1965.[7] Dr. Mondlane told Professor Burke that in African politics, there was nothing that could be referred to as a "tribe." In order to support his stand, Dr. Mondlane summarized an article from *The New York Times* describing an intense conflict between two groups. He then asked Professor Burke to name the warring tribes. After some thought and consideration, Professor Burke named two African tribes and gave support for his choices. Dr. Mondlane proved his point by revealing the fact that the energetic conflict was between Flemish and Walloon Belgians. Conclusions like the one by Professor Burke are not rare. If the Flemish and Walloon Belgians were African ethnic groups, most Westerners and many Africans would have consciously and unconsciously understood the entire conflict in terms of "tribalism" and "generations of tribal hatred." These concepts have been widely used in the past and continue to be used to explain too much, too simply. In order to identify and objectively analyze the cultural and political forces that have made certain political trends not just necessary but inevitable in Uganda, I have chosen to consider ethnic societies in neutral terms. The "ethnic societies" should correctly be treated as groups, interest groups and political interest groups.

I should at this juncture show that what is considered a tribe is not much more than what in other contexts might be referred to as "groups," "interest groups" or "political interest groups." According to Professor David B. Truman, for a number of people to be considered a group they must have shared attitudes or interests and must have relatively frequent interactions on the basis of their shared attitudes.[8] David Truman's definition of a group is restrictive in that there must be frequent interaction on the basis of shared interests, values or attitudes. Upon examination of the pre-colonial political systems and cultures of the African people, one cannot avoid the obvious conclusion that ethnic groups were and are today groups that function as interest groups and political interest groups. Ethnic political organizations, dances, food taboos, marriage ceremonies, common belief in supernatural, attitudes towards property, etc.--all form the bulk of shared attitudes and include a continuous flow of activities around those shared attitudes.

During the pre-colonial era these groups frequently functioned as interest groups. According to Professor Truman, an interest group is any group that, on the basis of one or more shared attitudes, makes certain claims upon other groups, for the establishment, maintenance or enhancement of forms of behaviors that are implied by the shared attitude.[9] As one examines the pre-colonial societies, he finds that ethnic groups conflicted with one another for land, animals, particular places considered to be of spiritual value, and, above all, to impose their own kind of political systems on their neighbors and to extract tribute from them. Each ethnic group had its unique common impulse of passions and interests--which directed and determined the style of conflict with their neighbors. Some of these groups gravitated towards war with their neighbors because they vehemently believed and supported their ambitious leaders who contended for preeminence, power and glory. After a critical examination of ethnic group actions and tendencies, one finds that groups like the Uganda Bar Association, Ku Klux Klan, labor organizations, American Medical Association, etc., are essentially the same as ethnic groups.

The point is that, by definition, "group" or "interest group" or "political interest group" have nothing to do with the reasons for which people associate in order to regularize and stabilize their kind of internal interactions and external relations. Group cohesion, exclusiveness and intensity of warmth among its members have a lot to do with group effectiveness but are of no consequence in terms of what can or cannot be identified and treated as an interest group or political interest group. Consequently, it is natural and sincere for me to say that I am proud of the fact that I am a Muganda (a member of Buganda ethnic group), and an ardent Uganda nationalist. In my opinion, it makes very little difference whether "Muganda" comes after or before "Uganda." The order depends on circumstances rather than strength of identity and depth of political loyalty. When I am in Uganda it makes sense to say that I am a "Muganda" for I assume that the person I am talking to knows that I am Ugandan. Outside of Uganda, it makes more sense to say I am "Ugandan" for "Muganda" would hardly make any sense to most people. It is like an American identifying himself as a Catholic and American or American and Catholic. Both Catholicism and Americanism can be integral aspects of the same person and saying "Catholic" before "American" does not necessarily mean that one is less American primarily because the United States government supports the use of the "pill." It should be recognized, therefore, that the main difference between ethnic groups and labor unions in the United States or Uganda, for instance, is that the two kinds of groups conflict with other groups for different values. The laborers' attitudes and interaction are based on the various and unequal distribution of property, whereas for the ethnic groups the basis of shared attitudes and interaction are the internally directed customs, traditional forms of government and past political experience. While the majority of Baganda (the people of the Buganda ethnic group) would like to vote for candidates who speak highly of their Kabaka, American labor union members tend to vote for those candidates less allied with big business and sympathetic to labor values and goals.

It seems to me that the political history of Uganda can best be understood as a history of conflicting groups: large and small ethnic groups, trying to promote or to protect themselves, their property and their values. Generalizations about ethnic politics in Uganda is of very limited help in one's attempt to understand and appreciate the political and social problems of Uganda's political environment. Individual ethnic cases vary so significantly that generalization can be unquestionably misleading. No two ethnic groups in Uganda have identical traditional political systems. No two ethnic groups can be said to have identical heritages of traditional social and political institutions. None of the ethnic groups I know have identical attitudes towards authority and leadership in the traditional sense.

Today very few ethnic groups in Uganda have the same base of economic, political and social resources. In spite of the vigorous nationalistic activities since independence, there remains dynamic diversity of ethnic group cultures. No two groups in Uganda can seriously be considered to be at the same level or stage of economic, political and educational development. The diversity of values, attitudes, traditional political systems and institutions in Uganda make a careful examination of some ethnic groups essential for one's attempt to understand the Ugandan political climate. As a manageable compromise between generalizations embracing all Ugandans and an analysis of each group, it shall suffice to deal with three traditional political systems. A close examination of these systems will provide us with the necessary background to evaluate the Ugandan colonial experience, its impact and whether a national consensus was or was not created by the time of independence.

Chiga - The People of Modern Kigezi District

The Chiga people were estimated to be about 100,000 by 1932-33. They have occupied the southeast corner of Uganda and for centuries cultivated the steep slopes of their beautiful mountains usually referred to as "the Switzerland of Uganda." They farm millet, corn, peas, beans and tend flocks of sheep and goats. In the fertile low grassy plains, many of them raise a considerable amount of cattle. Today the Chiga are well known in the urban areas of Uganda as industrious cultivators, whose district is progressively becoming the vegetable garden of Uganda.

The Chiga have cultural similarities with their neighbors. They speak a Bantu[10] language closely related to languages spoken by their neighbors in Bonyoro, Toro and Ankole. Similarities are also obvious in songs and dances exchanged back and forth, in the styles of their houses or huts, and in other customs like the polygamous patriarchal household, clan systems and veneration of ancestors. Unlike their neighbors, however, the Chiga have always had a highly decentralized social control system. In Ankole and Rwanda, the population is divided into distinct castes or classes. The peasants who are very much like the Chiga are ruled by a distinct pastoral people who are recognized as overlords and political conquerors. The pastoral people are actual rulers. As May Edel observed in 1932-33, the peasants are ruled "by pastoral overlords who in physical type as well as in their mode of life appear to be just what local legend calls them--a distinct, intrusive, conquering people."[11]

Unlike the people under divine kingship rule in Ankole and Rwanda, the Chiga were not a politically united people. They had no overlords and they had no authoritative units other than the basic family unit. They had internal conflicts and conflicts with their neighbors but never attempted to show a desire for centralization of authority. In spite of the fact that they were proud of being independent in spirit, they had a high degree of consensus. Their common customs, voluntary mutual obligations, common enjoyments of beer feasts, need for each other's assistance in matters of marriage, kinship bonds arising out of the exogamous marriage relationship, clan lines, and other factors forming a network of interpersonal relationship constituted the basis of their unity, distinctiveness and strength.

The history of the Chiga includes skirmishes with their neighbors. Chiefs of Rwanda and the Ankole Kingdom attempted many times to subjugate them and exact tribute from them. The Pygmy people, too, view the Chiga as fair game for attack and plunder. And the Pygmies' raids on Chiga country are described by May Edel as "terrible to the Chiga because they were entirely destructive."[12]

In spite of the apparent need for formal organization and common defense, the Chiga never set up a political system. Their high degree of consensus without government served as the sole basis of their unity to defend themselves from their neighbors. The Chiga, like most Bantu, had clans. But clans for the Chiga "had no unity beyond their common good taboo."[13] What May Edel observed about the social control of the Chiga is pretty much the same as the social control before British rule:

> There is no formal authority beyond that exercised by the father over his immediate household. . . .
>
> Sanctions are on the whole imposed on the principle of self-help by the individual or the group directly affected by some misconduct or failure to meet obligations, rather than by the kin group of the offender or by any neutral authority.[14]

The Chiga society was so consensual that the offended party's action was the law. Somehow their common political culture made community authority and a community police force unnecessary even in cases where arbitration was necessary, a hearing before a tribunal of respect, unpaid elders was arranged, but these almost regular court trials had no power to enforce decisions. Public opinion, disgrace and ridicule was the invincible secret force behind their decisions and made resort to violence in most cases unnecessary.

Much the same pattern was followed for very serious offenses.

> Offenses within the group have to be settled right there. No person external to it can have any other than a conciliatory role. . .
>
> Fratricide and incest for example are problems affecting only the close kin group, who are the ones actually injured. A man who has killed his brother is supposed to be put to death by his own father or brothers, traditionally he was buried alive with the corpse of his victim.[15]

It was these people--strong believers in their traditional ways and to whom "individualism" was a basis of their society--who were brought under effective British control with the help of Baganda, in a matter of years. The experience of these people under centralized authority and their traditional ways will enhance our understanding of the difficult problems of creating a national consensus during the colonial era.

The Karamojong: Social Organization and Social Control

The Chiga and the Karamojong are two interesting and excellent examples of the very varied peoples of Uganda. The Karamojong occupy the northeastern district of Karamoja. Theirs is a country of picturesque flat open plains into which an occasional rocky mountain or hill mass intrudes itself. Unlike the Chiga, the Karamojong are not "Bantu" and they are not farmers. They are Hamites who spend their lives watching herds of cattle and who occasionally spend their nights on bloody raids against their neighbors for cattle. In contrast to the chitter-chatter of the Chiga or the rich vowels of the Baganda, the Karamojong talk little.[16] With their nine-foot spears, their very able long, thin thighs can take them thirty to fifty miles on a raid at night for cattle. Cattle is much more than a means of survival. Cattle is the source of emotional satisfaction and the prerequisite for full social life. Karamojong values, attitudes and social organization, therefore, stress cattle possession, herding and protection. Consequently, herding is one of the most significant elements of the decentralized but authoritative political system of the Karamojong.

The Karamojong political community is a policy group which pursues particular values and actions based on the common interests of its members. Members of the community interact and have a strong sense of "oneness" on the basis of their commonly acknowledged individual rights, privileges and obligations. The "rights" and privileges include:

a) Right to graze and water one's cattle in any part of the Karamojong country without interference from other members of the political community.

b) Right to immediate assistance by members of the community, when a member conflicts or is in competition with outsiders.

c) Right to redress grievances against any other member of the political community.

d) Right to seize the cattle of non-members of the Karamojong community without being questioned by the community as to the motive or appropriateness of the action.

The "elders" monopolize the right to intercede with the deity to avert natural hazards and provide conditions in which stock, crops and people may prosper.

As in any other community the "rights" carried with them a number of obligations for the members of the political community.

a) Members were prohibited from seizing the stock of other members except for justifiable reasons.

b) Members were prohibited from fighting other Karamojong with spears.

c) Members were obligated to assist any other Karamojong in need. Assistance was to be given whenever requested.

d) Members were obligated to respect the elders and obey all the decisions the elders arrived at as a group.

The Karamojong regarded any violation of the rights, privileges and obligations as "wronging the community" which was punishable only by the orders of the elders. Neville Dyson-Hudson, after living with the Karamojong for 33 months in 1956-58, observed: "Such political rights may be expected by tribal birth or residence, but depend ultimately on commitment to the policies which the group pursues and which are its clearest defining features."[17] Hudson's observations make it clear that the political community was based primarily on group values and policies rather than on birth and residence. The full commitment of the members to the values and policies of the group is what made the Karamojong distinctive from other people and provided the consensus on which the political system was based. Commitment to Karamojong values and policies was a necessary condition for legitimate authority.

The social organization and allocation of authority were based on age. Adult males were organized in a series of groups based on age. According to Hudson, "Age organization provides both the source of political authority and the main field in which it is exercised among Karamojong."[18]

The age system was a finite series of age-based corporate groups interrelated in accordance with a set of general principles. An age group consisted of all males who happened to go through a common single initiation ceremony.[19] A single initiation ceremony was held within each five to six year period. Mr. Hudson uses the term "generation-set" for five age groups coming one after another.[20] The "generation-set," therefore, was a corporate group of wider time-span and larger membership. The oldest "generation-set" was the source of political leadership. The elders were respected and credited with wisdom in worldly matters. Besides having experienced life, they were the ones who had the ability and right to intercede with the deity for assistance. The elders made peace and war between Karamojong and outsiders. They also made all public decisions and were the only ones who could hand down authoritative decisions concerning individual conflicts within the community.

In a sense, age was a key to political power, but no power was vested in any single individual. Some elders were more influential than others but all decisions were group decisions. As Mr. Hudson pointed out:

> Cutting the matter is in the hands of the elders, who state a decision after hearing all who wish to speak. That decision is then binding on both parties who are sent off to settle their grievance in terms of it. No further action is taken by the elders unless the (by now acknowledged) plaintiff returns to complain that the decision has been ignored. In that case, the elders call on the young men to enforce their decision. . . .[21]

The assembly of elders was the legislature and the court of law. The society had no police agency but the decisions of the elders were always carried out. The elders' recognized ability to use the supernatural to enforce their decisions and the junior generation-set's obligation to carry out the elders' orders made it very easy to accomplish policies and enforce decisions. The Karamojong, whose political experience was decentralized authority acquired through age, were soon to live under colonial centralized authority whose basis was not common customs and attitudes but pure police force.

The Traditional Centralized Political System -- BUGANDA KINGDOM

The Buganda people, estimated to be over 3 million out of Uganda's population of 9-1/2 million, occupy one-fourth of the country. They were the shaping influence of Uganda during the period of British rule. They spread their agriculture and organization outward during the colonial period so that ethnic groups like the Langi, Acholi and Iteso practically abandoned pastoralism to become cultivators on the Baganda's model. In spite of their shaping influence and free and valuable participation in colonial politics, the Baganda remained indifferent to national issues and infinitely loyal to their traditional political system.

The hierarchical political system of the Buganda Kingdom was a merit system where excellence in war, demonstration of administrative ability and personal acquaintance with the king were the key to high office in the power hierarchy. Pages were sent to the king's court by clan elders, chiefs and ordinary citizens. Any page who demonstrated administrative abilities and loyalty to the Kabaka and who was agreeable to the king's eye could be appointed to office. Power was accessible to pages as long as their services pleased the king. Good leadership and absolute loyalty to the throne meant high office or higher office--making a hierarchical political system where the Kabaka was the patron and all chiefs and subjects were clients in the full sense.

The political organization of Buganda needs closer and more careful examination

The Pre-Colonial Period : 33

because by virtue of its efficient centralized organization, Buganda became the cornerstone of British indirect rule in Uganda. The political system of Buganda before the arrival of Europeans in the country can be summarized in a form of a diagram.

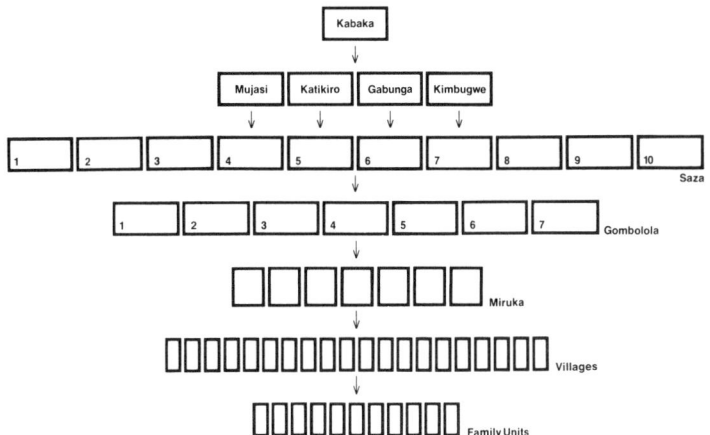

The ultimate source of power and justice in the political hierarchy was the Kabaka. Under the Kabaka were the most important chiefs in the kingdom. Katikiro occupied and served the role of a prime minister. The other most important chiefs and Saza chief met as a legislative council but no decisions were authoritative without the personal approval of the Kabaka. The Katikiro had traditionally been the commander-in-chief of the Kabaka's army but when larger armies were raised in the 1870's in preparation for territorial expansion, Kabaka Mutesa I established a separate department of the armed forces under the specialized leadership provided by the king's appointed official whose title was MUJASI.

Gabunga was one of the most important chiefs. He was the admiral of Buganda's navy on Lake Victoria--a navy that expanded the Buganda Kingdom all along the lakeshore towards Ankole. Among the important chiefs was the king's treasurer who was also treasurer of the kingdom as a whole. Kimbugwe was a household figure of the king, whose responsibility was to take charge of the Kabaka's umbilical cord--an object of great religious veneration in Buganda.

Below the most important chiefs were the ten Saza (county) chiefs. The Buganda Kingdom was divided into ten administrative territorial units--each unit was administered by a Saza chief. The Saza chiefs, like the most important chiefs, were personal appointees of the Kabaka, and they held their offices at the Kabaka's pleasure.

The Sazas (counties) were in turn divided into small administrative units, each unit was called a Gombolola (sub-county) and each Gombolola was also divided into small administrative units called Miruka (Parish). Each Parish had its own chief. Under the Parish chief were the villages, each of which was led by a chief (Mutongola). A village consisted of about 100 to 1000 people and was the smallest political unit; each village had a court that settled most of the disputes between members of the village or members of the village accused by a member of another village. Membership to a village was based on residence. Parties to a case were free to appeal to higher courts in the hierarchy. From village court to Parish court, then to sub-county courts, to Saza court, to the Council of Saza chiefs and the most important chiefs. The supreme court was the Kabaka himself. Defiance or criticism of the Kabaka's decision could mean immediate execution.

Before British rule, the Buganda Kingdom was divided into administrative units, but none of the units existed or functioned independently. All political units were administered in the name of the Kabaka. Consequently:

> Chiefs reflected delegations of authority in their favor but had none in their own right. Although political groupings were territorial they did not become solidary associations with independent attachment to local figures. The relationship of the citizen was to his king. The relationship to the chief depended on the latters position as king's lieutenant.[22]

Legitimacy in Buganda was inherent in the Kabaka. The Kabaka personally appointed all the most important chiefs, the Saza chiefs, and the Gombolola chiers. At the pleasure of the Kabaka, chiefs were promoted, demoted, transferred, retired, removed from office or even beheaded. The Kabaka was the fountain of authority and justice and his authority was real and felt in every household. Regarding chiefs, Mr. Apter stated that, "Whatever his position in the hierarchy, each chief holds his mandate from the Kabaka, but subordinate chiefs serve the chief next higher in the echelon."23

The village chiefs (Batongole) were the personal assistants of the Kabaka in each village. Their presence and intimate association with the affairs of the village life made the Kabaka's presence real. Orders from a chief were regarded as orders from the Kabaka by all Baganda below the chief's position in the hierarchy. Direct contact with chiefs--particularly chiefs high enough in the hierarchy--provided, in the minds of the people, a direct contact with the Kabaka.

Strengthening the Kabaka's actual political and psychological hold on the people were the scattered estates of the Kabaka. Estates were the Kabaka's private patrimony scattered throughout the various counties. The Kabaka's deputies and personal friends who controlled the estates provided further contact with the ordinary citizens in whose minds, the Kabaka's land and Kabaka's men were the actual representation of the king himself. The Kabaka was also brought closer to the people by the custom of moving the Kabaka's residence periodically to different locations in the kingdom. Besides bringing the Kabaka to the people, shifting the Kabaka's capital served other purposes.

> Since it was customary to shift the capital of the Kabaka and there was no fixed locale for his residence, the roving quality of his authority further emphasized the fact that boundaries between Sazas were simply administrative conveniences and not local solidary groupings.24

As a result of the arrangement, all citizen allegiances were directly attached to the Kabaka and indirectly to him through chiefs. All chiefs were the Kabaka's appointees, and all were exclusively responsible to the Kabaka, while serving chiefs higher than themselves in the hierarchy. Allegiance attached to the chief was therefore allegiance attached to the Kabaka. The arrangement made the entire kingdom effectively controlled by the Kabaka and the Kabaka's authority was supreme.

Besides the Kabaka's monopoly of political power, the Kabaka had considerable control and influence on purely social organization. Kabaka was Sabataka--the head of all the clans. Every Muganda was a clan member and proudly owed social allegiance to his clan. The clan leadership was the court of appeal for all cases involved with burial rights, inheritance of land and personal belongings (wills), and land ownership cases of the clan members. But the Kabaka was the head of all clan heads and served as the final court of appeal. Parties to a case involving clan members, members of different clans or clans themselves could appeal to the Kabaka and the Kabaka's decision was binding and final.

The clan leaders were also religious and customary figures. One of their most important duties was to watch over the graves of the clan since Baganda valued and considered the dead to be living with them. Clan leaders were also very important religious figures, but even their religious authority was also like other authorities in the kingdom based on the clan leader's relationship with the Kabaka.

The political system and social organization of Buganda were such that the political, social and religious life of the people were interlocked in the person of the Kabaka--making the Kabaka an all inclusive supreme law of the Baganda.

Unquestionably, the social organizations and controls of the Chiga, Karamojong and Baganda makes one aware of the sharp contrast between the political attitudes that existed before colonial rule. The political and social systems described are radically different from each other in structure, source of authority and functions. The hierarchical chieftancy in Buganda, for instance, was highly geared towards taxation, massive mobilization for war and specialization of leadership in army and navy in preparation for territorial expansion of Buganda at the expense of her neighbors. Most important is the fact that even where numerous similarities between traditional political organization existed, there were politically critical differences. Namely, Ankole, Toro, and Bunyoro (Kitara) were kingdoms like Buganda. But none of the kings had as much political power as the Kabaka, and the kingdoms themselves were not effectively centralized states like Buganda.

In Buganda there were defined ranks based on the number of people a chief administered on behalf of the Kabaka. There was no class system in Buganda. The system was so open that slaves could (and some did) rise and fall within the power hierarchy, depending on their personal relationship with the Kabaka and their ability in matters of leadership. Unlike in Buganda, in Ankole and Bunyoro (Kitara) the population was culturally, politically and economically divided between a ruling class (the Hima and Babito) and the commoners (the Beiru and Hutu). The class system lines were almost impossible to cross by traditional political means.

It was these ethnic groups whose political and social experiences and ethos were radically different, and in some cases contradictory, for which national arbitrary boundaries were to be drawn (1880-1886) in accordance with the political aims of Britain in the area.

The manner in which these politically and socially independent ethnic groups were to be compelled into a political union is the subject of the next chapter. It should be noted here, that the ethnic group adaptation and maladaptation to the imposed union and colonial administration were largely dependent on the political history of the group.

Historically, there was no evidence that two or more of these groups had ever made an alliance for common defense or for economic or social purposes. No group had ever considered certain values as a common concern. Consequently, for many centuries there had been no unifying group interaction except for group conflicts over territory, animals, water and occasionally women. Equally important was the fact that the political system of Buganda soon proved to be inherently flexible, adaptive and highly efficient. Approval or acquiescence by the Kabaka in principle, and fact meant approval and acquiescence by the kingdom as a whole. Since it was Mutesa I, Kabaka of Buganda, who had personally requested the Europeans to come to Buganda, Buganda was soon to become the classical example of British indirect rule in the colonial political history of Uganda.

2

The Colonial Experience

The British Takeover and Buganda's Sub-Imperialism

Buganda Kingdom was well known along the East African coast long before the coming of Europeans. The Arabs from Zanzibar had been trading with Buganda for some time before colonization. Owing to trade contact and stories told about the Buganda Kingdom, the coastal people regarded Buganda as, "A nascent African kingdom, powerful and virile and quite without peer in East Africa."[1]

The Arabs had carried on considerable trade with Kabaka Suna (1832-1857). There were legends of wonderful gifts his highness, the Sultan of Zanzibar, Seyyid Majid bin Said, sent to Buganda and the cordial relationship that prevailed between the two states during and after Suna's reign.

According to Sir John Gray, the Sultan sent a caravan to Buganda in 1869 bearing gifts for Kabaka Mutesa I. Kabaka Mutesa I, the successor to Suna, anxious to expand trade with the coast, returned the compliment with gifts of ivory.[2] It is very important to note that at that time Mutesa I was in the process of militantly expanding the kingdom, particularly at the expense of Bunyoro Kingdom. Meanwhile, small kingdoms like Koki voluntarily affiliated themselves with Buganda to avoid military conflicts with and conquest by Buganda. At that time, Zanzibar was not only the armies' supplier to Buganda, but also her trade with Buganda was essential for Buganda's vision and aim for a larger, more powerful Buganda Kingdom.

> Buganda was a state geared to war. But war and conquest were not the only occupations. Commerce brought in by Arab traders moved along well-demarcated routes. There were trading depots at way stations inland from the coast. Arab factors carried on a flourishing exchange in slaves, ivory, cloth and manufactured implements. African chiefs and headmen were paid tribute in return for transit and trading privilege.[3]

Mutesa I and the chiefs were profiting from the trade which made internal order and stability in Buganda necessary, but most importantly they wanted to expand trade activities. As one missionary came to point out in the 1880's, the Kabaka of Buganda, Mutesa I, kept a permanent army and navy of more than 6000 men engaged in occasional skirmishes with neighboring people in search of slaves and political order within and outside the Buganda Kingdom. Mackay, one of the earliest of the church missionary society representatives in East Africa, described the situation thus:

> If traders were to find secure trade and transit conditions along the routes to the coast, they needed control and protection. If wealthy tribes like Buganda or Nyanwezi found their income prejudiced because of the disorderliness of adjacent tribes expeditions would result and hegemony extended over unpoliced areas.[4]

In short, by the time of European arrival in East Africa, Buganda was the largest and mightiest African political system in East Africa. Besides being the most powerful political organization, Buganda was in the process of expanding her territory at the expense of her neighbors, particularly Bunyoro Kingdom. Mutesa I was soon to invite the Europeans to come to his kingdom and eventually to use British assistance in his ambition for trade and territorial expansion.

In search of the source of the Nile, the British explorer John Hanning Speke became the first European to set foot on the soil of Buganda. Captain John Speke entered the region now called Uganda in 1862. As Speke made his way into Buganda (1858-

1862) from the East African coast, another route into Uganda was being developed by Sir Samuel Baker, pushing his way southward from the Sudan. Baker made contact with Kamurasi, the Omukama (king) of Bunyoro, but no friendly relationship developed. Baker, as governor of the Equatorial Province for the Khedive, was soon to make the first military attempt to bring the Bunyoro Kingdom under Egyptian domination. Sudan already was under Egyptian rule. The attempt led to hostility and to the Bunyoro Kingdom's resistance to European influence. Bunyoro Kingdom had been the most powerful and extensive kingdom in the area for two hundred years. Bunyoro's military victory over Baker's army and her past glory made the Banyoro (people of Bunyoro Kingdom) more determined to resist European influence and control.

Speke and Baker met at Gondakoro, which meant that two routes into Uganda had been established: one from the Sudan and the other from Zanzibar. The attitudes and experience of Speke and Baker towards the people whom they met in Uganda were soon to influence British colonial policies in Uganda and shape the nature of political control over Uganda. The impressions of Speke as recorded in J. H. Speke's journal of the discovery of the source of the Nile, are well summed up by Professor Kenneth Ingham.[5]

> On first setting foot in Uganda in 1862, John Hanning Speke, soldier, geographer and explorer, might have been inclined to believe some of those stories of a golden age. For having left

behind the tribes to the south of
Lake Victoria harassed by slavers
and enslaved by superstition, he
was filled with delight at the
"quiescent beauty" and apparent
orderliness of southern Uganda,
the straight wide roads, broad
as an English coach road, which
cut through the long grass and
climbed the many hills were in
strange contrast to the wretched
tracks in all the adjacent districts. The huts of the in-
habitants and the gardens too
were clean and neat that no fault
could be found with them. And
this was but the doorway to the
Kingdom of Buganda. . . .

As he approached the capital, near
the site on which Kampala now
stands, Speke could not restrain
his surprise and pleasure at the
fine appearance of the people
lined the road to see him.[6]

It was a custom of long standing in
Buganda to line the road to see a digni-
fied visitor arrive. Speke was highly impressed by the social and political organization of Buganda. Above all, he was very
moved by the friendly and impressive re-
ception extended to him by Mutesa I and his
people.

> I cut a poor figure in the
> comparison with the display
> of the dressy Waganda. They
> wore neat bark cloth cloaks
> resembling the best yellow
> corduroy cloth, crimp and

well set, as if stiffened with
starch, and over that as upper-
cloaks, a patch work of small
antelope skins, which I observed
were sewn together as well as any
English glovers could have pieced
them; whilst their head-dresses,
generally were abrus turbans, set
off with highly polished boartusks,
stick-charms, seeds, beads or
shells. . . .7

On his return to Britian, Speke argued that Buganda was ripe for missionary activities but the missionary societies still preferred to work slowly from the East African coast towards the interior. Meanwhile, Baker continued in his service as governor of the Equatorial Province. In 1871 he returned to Bunyoro, raised an Egyptian flag at Gondakoro and issued a proclamation on May 26 abolishing the slave trade in the region and annexing Bunyoro territory to Egypt. In 1872 the Bunyoro Kingdom rose against Baker and his Egyptian troops and militarily forced Baker out of the kingdom. Bunyoro, after her second military victory over Baker, became more determined to resort to war to keep the Egyptians and English out of her territory.

During this time another European reached Buganda from the East African coast. Henry Morton Stanley, who had been sent on a journalistic expedition across Africa by *The New York Herald* and *London Daily Telegraph*, reached Mutesa I's capital in April, 1875.

To Mutesa the arrival of Stanley seemed most opportune in view of

the disturbing interest which the
Egyptian government was showing
in Buganda. Stanley in his turn
was considerably impressed by
Mutesa not only a man whose interest in religion might easily
be aroused but also a ruler strong
enough to ensure the orderly government under which peaceful
evangelization might take place.
Many long discussions concerning
the Christian faith occupied
Stanley's time during his stay
with Mutesa and the latter eventually agreed to a request being
sent to England for missionaries
to visit his kingdom.[8]

The message from Mutesa requesting missionaries to be sent to Buganda was soon
sent by Stanley. The letter was published
in the *Daily Telegraph* on November 15, 1875.
Fortunately, or unfortunately, the letter
was met with considerable enthusiasm compared to Speke's opinions, eleven years
earlier. Stanley, like Speke, was impressed by the Buganda Kingdom and her people. The highly diplomatic and friendly
way in which Buganda handled her first contacts with the Europeans was soon to give a
special role to Buganda in the colonization
and colonial administration of Uganda.

The Kabaka's request for missionaries
received positive response. The Church
Missionary Society sent a group of Protestant missionaries led by Alexander Mackay.
Mackay and company arrived in Buganda in
1878. Soon the Protestant missionaries
were followed by French Catholics. Mutesa
I, as the story goes, had a number of wives

and he knew how to satisfy them all, but almost immediately it became clear that his ability to appease and satisfy was overtaxed by the three religious groups at his court. Arabs (Islam), Catholics and Portestants were ungracefully contending for the Kabaka's favor. Soon afterwards the Kabaka found himself confronted with the worst civil conflicts. But the Kabaka continued to play one group against the other. This approach did not succeed for long. European missionaries were followed by merchants in the form of the Imperial British East Africa Company--a group of English traders who were more inclined to identify themselves with philanthropy rather than commerce. In cases of social disorder disrupting trade, the traders pushed for British formal undertakings of colonial acquisition.

Mutesa I soon realized his difficult position. He had known the Arabs longer and he had profited from Buganda's trade with Zanzibar. He needed an alliance with the British, for the Egyptians had attempted to annex Bunyoro and their troops were still near Buganda's northern frontier. At the same time, the British were not to be trusted, for Britain and Egypt were allies. Seeing that British Protestants and French Catholics were more hostile to each other than to the Arabs, Mutesa I deemed it prudent to maintain them as potential enemies to check each other's influence. But Mutesa I died in 1884 and after his death, Buganda plunged into civil religious wars over the succession to the throne. The Catholics and Protestants were determined to see the influence of Islam curtailed. They were definitely not prepared to accept a Moslem king.

Mwanga, Mutesa I's successor, soon became tired of the religious conflicts and disliked the missionaries who were trying to control the selection of pages to the Kabaka's court which meant indirectly selecting future chiefs. From 1885-1887 Mwanga had martyred about 20 Catholics and 15 Protestants for challenging his authority. Soon afterwards, Mwanga became strongly opposed to all foreign religious influence.

> Mwanga was determined to rid himself of all who were not pagans. In April, 1888, he tried to destroy Arab, Catholic and Protestant groups by leaving them on an island where they would starve to death. The readers, refusing to embark in canoes and ignoring the commands of the king organized a revolution: entirely successful it resulted in Mwanga fleeing the throne.[9]

The religious competition for influence resulted in conflicts and religious wars which plunged Buganda into a state of social disorder. The disorders meant economic disaster for the trading companies which argued that British political control of Buganda was necessary. On September 3, 1888, the Imperial British East Africa Company (IBEAC) received a royal charter from Lord Salisbury's government with instructions to preserve law and order in Buganda. However, the religious conflicts continued. The Christians (Europeans) united and successfully curtailed the Arab influence but soon they began to fight each other. Meanwhile, business declined and finally the Imperial British

East Africa Company decided to withdraw from Buganda. The religious wars (1884-1889) made the political realities clear to both Buganda and Britain. The Kabaka of Buganda could not successfully contain the religious conflicts. The Kabaka had to make allies with one of the religious groups and tame the other groups. To the British, the experience with the IBEAC was a warning. Law and order in Buganda would not only be very difficult to maintain but also too costly without a Kabaka.

With the pending IBEAC withdrawing from Uganda, Britain was faced with two alternatives. A British withdrawal from Uganda was one alternative but an unacceptable one. Britain had to take over Uganda, for as stated by the British Foreign Office in the cabinet memorandum of September 7, 1892, Britain deemed it necessary to take political control of Uganda. "When we gave a charter to the IBEAC, we understood that its main idea was to push up to Uganda. The aim had been to take Uganda, and so prevent the Germans from linking up their West Coast sphere across the upper Nile to their East African possessions."10

The British were neither willing to leave Uganda alone nor willing to spend money on the administration of Uganda. It should be noted that before the company made a decision to withdraw their agents from Buganda in July, 1891, they had made several appeals to Britain for a railway subsidy and funds to cover some administrative costs. In May, 1891, the prime minister himself publicly declared his deep interest in an Uganda railway. But the House of Commons and the Cabinet continued to vote down bills aimed at helping the company out of her financial difficulty.¹¹ The majority in Parliament was against a foreign office takeover after the company's withdrawal. Majority opinion at the time was well-summed up in the following:

> What possible reasons could be found for holding Uganda? Is it trade? There is no traffic. Is it religion? The Catholics and Protestants . . . are occupied in nothing but cutting each others throats. Is it slavery? There is no evidence that there is any slave trade in question in this region. . . . I see nothing but endless expense, trouble and disaster in prospect if we allow ourselves to drift into any sort of responsibility for this business. . . .¹²

Britain was to spend no money on the administration of Uganda but could not leave Uganda to the Germans. Concern over administrative cost and Mwanga's realization that Buganda could not be ruled without an alliance with one of the religious groups was soon to be the basis of mutual cooperation and assistance between Buganda and Britain in the colonization of Uganda. The alliance between Buganda and colonial officials marked the beginning of British rule in Uganda. However, the British were to become increasingly dependent on Baganda chiefs and Buganda political institutions for the administration of the country.

> The first years of British over-
> rule in Buganda seem, in retro-
> spect, to have been a honeymoon
> period. . . . For a government
> which had to pacify a country
> with a handful of white admini-
> strators, to build roads and of-
> fices, to introduce cash crops
> and to raise revenues, there was
> obviously no more efficient
> tribal structures than a monarchy,
> ruling through a hierarchy of
> administrative chiefs who like
> the British, but unlike some of
> the surrounding tribes, under-
> stood what was meant by execu-
> tive authority.[13]

With British military assistance, the Protestants in Buganda defeated the Catholics in a battle at Mengo in 1892, marking the beginning of a mutual relationship between British interests and Protestant leadership in Buganda.[14] Apolo Kwaga, an Anglican prime minister who had led the Protestant forces to victory, remained prime minister. From this point on, leadership in Buganda was to be dominated by Protestants. The Kabaka was a Protestant and so was the prime minister. Finally, an alliance with Britain was in order. The unwritten conditions for the alliance were such that the Kabaka would help in the establishment of a British protectorate. In return Britain would not only recognize the Kabaka's traditional roles but also assist Buganda in her conflicts with her neighbors.

Once the British were established in Buganda, their preferred method of consolidating their position on the upper Nile was simply to enlarge Buganda. As a result, between 1894 and 1900, Buganda obtained control of further territory on its western borders, over southern Bunyoro and over the Buvuma islands. : . .[15]

Buganda had returned to her original state of law and order immediately after the end of the religious wars in 1892. The kingdom used the British in her own interests--for a larger, more powerful Buganda Kingdom. The British, particularly Mr. Johnson, believed that Buganda Kingdom was destined to play a principal role in the administration of the protectorate within and outside Buganda.[16] As a result of Buganda's desire for territorial expansion and British favorable attitudes towards Buganda's political system, Buganda came to be a real power group within the protectorate--a group that had influence not only over other Africans but also over the British. Thus the consequences of Buganda's influence were "less emphasized, but intimately related to her internal continuity, is the perpetuation of Baganda's imperialistic past, especially in the guise of Ganda participation in the extension of British influence throughout the protectorate of Uganda."[17]

Buganda was not only prepared to assist the British but often suggested what particular actions should be taken against her neighbors resisting British influence. By assisting the British, particularly in their conflicts with the Bunyoro Kingdom, Buganda maintained her institutions and also secured a favorable position from which she managed to impose her political and social institutions on the other people in Uganda. Buganda was soon to become a real sub-imperialist state within the protectorate of Uganda, and a classical case of British indirect rule.

As a result of British collaboration with Buganda, the Uganda protectorate came into existence. The 1900 Buganda Agreement formalized the relationship between Buganda and Britain.[18] It is very important to note that at the time of the agreement, Buganda had already militarily acquired new territory. The 1900 Agreement not only legalized Buganda's acquisition of territory, but also transferred to Buganda five counties and parts of two other counties of the Bunyoro Kingdom. The counties were transferred to Buganda Kingdom in recognition of Buganda's considerable assistance to the British in their military campaign to subdue the Kingdom of Bunyoro. The counties became known as the "Lost Counties" and continued as a source of conflict and jealousy between Buganda and Bunyoro. The "Lost Counties" issue did not only persist throughout the colonial period and dominate a large part of the London conference for the Uganda independence constitution, but also proved to be the main threat to national unity immediately after independence.

Buganda Kingdom consisted of ten counties by 1884. Six years later, Buganda had 20 counties as a result of her newly acquired territories and the Uganda Agreement of 1900. Most people acquainted with Africa recognized the serious problems inherited from colonial domination--the problems of the artificial boundaries which cut

across major ethnic groups. Arbitrary
boundary problems in terms of African inter-state relations were well recognized,
because, since 1962, we have seen bloody
conflicts created by these boundaries
(northern Uganda versus southern Sudan
and northern Kenya versus Somaliland).
Some attention ought to be directed towards
the problems of boundaries in terms of the
internal political composition of an African state. As we shall see later, in the
case of Uganda, the boundaries not only
forced together groups which had been for
centuries political and social rivals but
also added fuel to the boundary conflicts
before stifling them. This action immediately after independence, made democratic government unpractical.

The Politics of Indirect Rule

Britain had successfully used Buganda
Kingdom to extend British control over her
neighbors, particularly the Bunyoro Kingdom. Buganda, too, had successfully used
British help and influence to expand her
territory and to preserve her own institutions. But most significant to note is
the fact that Britain was going to depend
on Buganda for the administration of most
parts of Uganda. The British, represented
by Sir Harry Johnston, were very anxious
to come to an arrangement that would involve very little active interference and
as little expense as possible on their
part. At the same time, Buganda Kingdom,
already pleased with her newly acquired
political and military supremacy over her
western rival, Bunyoro Kingdom, was very
willing to make available competent men,

accustomed to the exercise of power, who for many years became willing agents and profiteers of British authority and policies in much of Uganda.

> With the formation of the Lukiiko, or gathering of the more important chiefs, as a council of defined membership and regular sessions, Buganda offered the British a model for native administrations such as they had not encountered elsewhere in Africa.[19]

Britain, unwilling to spend money on the administration of Uganda, did not hesitate to rely on the efficient well-disciplined centralized political system of Buganda and Baganda chiefs. Mr. Johnston, the British representative in Uganda, appointed Kakunguru, a prince of the Buganda Kingdom, to administer western Bukedi country in Buganda style. Kakunguru took the opportunity to demonstrate his ability in military activities and public administration. He fought and defeated the Sudanese and Banyoro Nationalists who were still determined to repel British domination. According to Mr. Roberts, Kakunguru, with Sir Johnston's approval, did not confine his authority to Bukedi country. He advanced through Teso to the slopes of Mount Elgon.

At this point Mr. Johnston incautiously told Kakunguru that he would make him Kabaka (king) of Bukedi. Taking Johnston at his word, Kakunguru, as a prince of Buganda, found it very natural to divide the country between Teso and Mount Elgon into twenty counties which he administered on the pattern of post-1900

Buganda political style.[20] A few years
later Kakunguru was transferred to Busoga
where he transformed the political system
into a Buganda-style hierarchy. Before his
death Kakunguru had exercised his authority
in northern Bunyoro, Bukedi, Teso, Lango
and Busoga. Wherever he had been he left
Baganda chiefs in various positions of
power.

Meanwhile, on government orders, James
Miti, a Muganda chief, was sent into Bunyoro where he settled to divide up the country into administrative units as in Buganda.
Miti became county chief in Bunyoro and his
Baganda followers also obtained chieftainships. The Baganda chiefs in Bunyoro, like
elsewhere in Teso, Busoga, Bukedi and
Lango, served as judicial officials as
well as poll tax collectors and general
administrators for the local governments
as well as the central government. By
1910 Baganda chiefs had ruled in Kigazi,
Toro, Bankole, Bunyoro, Lango, Teso, Bugisu,
Busoga and Bukedi. The political colonial
experience of Uganda was of a pattern of
government by agreement between the British
and the Baganda. Most importantly, it was
the Baganda who did the greatest work--in
extending British and Buganda institutions
to the rest of Uganda.

As elsewhere in Africa, the ethnic
groups in Uganda resisted foreign domination. However, no two groups combined to
provide a unified resistance. Unlike the
case of Kenya or Tanzania, resistance to
colonial rule in Uganda, was not only resistance to British rule but to Baganda
rule in particular. In Kenya for instance,
the white settlers were the people most
legally concerned with land, labor, roads

and law and order. In Uganda, Buganda chiefs were the champions of land reforms, road building, labor matters and law and order.

The traditional political system in Buganda was geared to war as well as economic activities. The senior chiefs in Buganda, like the king, had estates in their respective areas of administration. The Uganda Agreement recognized the right to these estates and in the process enhanced the power and status of Baganda county chiefs. The Uganda Agreement of 1900 distributed 8,000 square miles (in Buganda alone) among 100 chiefs, giving Baganda chiefs and notables a double hold on the masses.

Traditionary Saza chiefs received no salaries. The reward for their services was mainly what they collected from the peasants on their estates. It should be noted that county chiefs received no salaries or wages for their administrative services until the 1930's. In 1922, for instance, peasants in Buganda through the Federation of Bataka, complained to the Kabaka that they were being over-taxed and forced to allot most of their land to growing cotton. The chiefs not only rejected the peasant petitions but passed a Lukiiko law in 1926 forcing Baganda peasants to give between 20 per cent and 35 per cent of their cotton crops to their landlords, plus 10 per cent of all other products.[21]

The chiefs paid themselves by taxing the peasantry. It was therefore in the interest of these chiefs to impose cotton growing and other cash crop cultivation in

Buganda and outside of Buganda. A. D. Roberts sums up Baganda chief activities outside Buganda as:

> Their handfuls of followers unpaid, but armed with guns or rifles, were usually, though by no means always enough to prevent forcible resistance to often harshly imposed innovations. They upheld the authority of chiefs who, acting on the agents' instructions, had now to collect taxes, recruit road gangs, enforce the storage of famine reserves and gain acceptance as arbitrators among people who had never acknowledged their authority. Moreover, the agents were largely responsible for the remarkable speed with which cotton growing was taken up; and Asian traders were not slow to establish themselves whenever Baganda posts assured them some security.[22]

In a sense Baganda chiefs became the forerunners of land reforms in most parts of Uganda. Like elsewhere in Africa, Africans resisted land reforms and the forced growing of cash crops. Whereas the African resistance was directed towards the settlers in Kenya and Germans in Tanganyika, the resistance in Uganda was in most cases directed towards Baganda chiefs who had a sizeable share in the cash crop business. Baganda chiefs were also the tax collectors and road gang recruiters for their own counties as well as for the central government. This meant that whereas in countries like Kenya, the tension resulting from foreign political control and compulsory new innovations was later to be condensed in the terms; down with the British and to hell with the missionaries; the three of which can be put in one package--to hell with the white man.

In Uganda, colonial rule before 1930 not only amplified the old tensions between Buganda and her neighbors, but also created new and more serious tensions. Buganda helped the British to defeat the Bunyoro Kingdom, took territory from her neighbors and the chiefs were the tax collectors and imposers of compulsory economic innovations. There were no white settlers in Uganda, therefore, most of the people's contact with colonial government was direct contact with Baganda chiefs. Consequently, most of the hostility and resentment of colonial policy and foreign administration was resentment and hostility directed at the chiefs outside the Buganda Kingdom. It was this understandable hostility and resentment of the Baganda outside of Buganda that made the politics of independence very difficult and the creation of a national consensus a formidable task. While in Kenya, the independence struggle was based on "down with the white man," in Uganda, the struggle was expressed in terms of "down with the British administrators and partially down with Buganda political domination."

According to Mr. Roberts' observation one can say that some Baganda chiefs did sterling work in encouraging cash crop cultivation in and outside of Buganda. But the continuous influx of Baganda into neighboring ethnic group areas and their obtaining of chieftainships which enabled them to impose their language, customs and

Christianity on the local people created
conflicts, hostility and resentment unavoidable.[23]

Besides the political and economic impact of the Baganda outside of Buganda
Kingdom, their influence was strongly reinforced by the Christian missions which relied heavily on Baganda catechists. Between 1909 and 1911, eighty-five Protestant Baganda teachers volunteered to go to
Teso, where Catholic catechists from Buganda had been at work as early as 1903.
Soon the Baganda were to look at themselves
as the leading political, economic and cultural reformers of Uganda. By 1933 in
Kigezi District, for instance, there were
no Europeans other than a few government
officers. But for many years before 1930,
Baganda chiefs (agents) and catechists
had established local courts under Baganda
chiefs to affect law and order in the
district.

Baganda chiefs not only administered
the district, collected head-tax and
changed traditional marriage arrangements
through forced limitation of bride-price
payments, but also put into effect a comprehensive ban on traditional religious
practices. The colonial officers declared the whole cult of Nyabingi Spirits
a subversive secret society. Baganda
chiefs carried out the capture and court
trials of its practitioners, many of
whom were sent to Kampala to serve prison
terms. The Chiga, as a people who recognized no authority beyond that of the
household-head, found themselves compelled
to comply to the Baganda's harsly imposed
new political, economic and religious innovations. Christianity flourished in

Kigezi and church dues and head-taxes were paid. Actual hostility and resentment against Baganda in Kigezi district became an aspect of the Uganda political environment that was to persist to this day.

In spite of resistance to Baganda chiefs and the British administration's harshly imposed political, economic and cultural innovations in most parts of Uganda, positive changes took place. By 1930, coffee, cotton and tea were grown in relatively large quantities in Uganda. Tea growing in Uganda started in 1903. The first recorded export of tea from Uganda was in 1929. By 1951, production of tea was 4,297,000 pounds and by 1961 production was at 11,278,158 pounds. Baganda had grown and cultivated small plots of coffee before the British arrival in Buganda. But commercial production of coffee (Arabica) began in 1900. In 1920, 20,783 acres of land were Arabica coffee gardens and by 1935, 19,279 acres were covered with Robusta coffee trees. The first official introduction of cotton was in 1903. Production for 1907 was 2,000 bales. By the mid-twenties the total produced in Uganda was about 200,000 bales and the 1937-1938 season production was 418,000 bales.[24]

As a result of cash crop growing, British officials in Uganda found themselves in a position to pay for the administration of Uganda. The role of the Kabaka and Kabaka's chief in Buganda were to remain the same in Buganda Kingdom. But the Baganda chiefs' administrative services outside of Buganda were no longer necessary. The British, at last, were in a position to pay for the policing of Uganda rather than relying on the Buganda Kingdom and Buganda's political system of self-paid chiefs. The role of Baganda chiefs outside of Buganda declined. However, the Baganda were going to continue to be the object of resentment and envy, mixed with admiration, outside Buganda throughout the colonial period as well as after independence.

Much of what has been pointed out so far seems to put too much emphasis on the Buganda Kingdom. In order to pinpoint the most critical issues in Uganda's political environment, it seems to me, that one has to have a good understanding of Buganda's history. The most significant forces behind what has happened since the beginning of the struggle for independence have been forces directly linked to what Baganda think of themselves and what non-Baganda think of Baganda.

Buganda is vitally important to Uganda politics for a number of reasons: Buganda region is equal in size to a quarter of the whole country and the Baganda constitutes about one-third of Uganda's population which is made up of more than 20 major ethnic groups. Furthermore, as of Independence Day, October 9, 1962, the Baganda held three-quarters of the civil service positions in Uganda and made up 50 per cent of the Ugandan educated elite. The top African leadership in the Muslim group, Roman Catholic church and Protestant church has always been occupied by Baganda. In addition, Kampala (situated in Buganda), the commercial and political capital of Uganda, is the location for the national industrial center and Makerere University College. Most teacher training colleges, technical schools and Uganda's international airport (Entebbe) are also located in Buganda. In short, whatever happens in Buganda, the feelings of Baganda towards themselves and in particular the feelings towards Baganda outside Buganda, have very significant implications for the entire Ugandan political system.

There are, however, forces of hostility and resentment towards the government in Uganda that have nothing to do with Buganda. It would be too long a task to trace these forces within each ethnic group in Uganda. It is sufficient for the purpose of this study to examine the colonial experience of Karamoja District and Toro Kingdom in addition to what we have already seen in connection with Buganda.

Karamoja District

The first contact between the Karamojong and the British came in 1898 when a military expedition led by Major J. MacDonald marched through the Karamoja country towards the Nile. British policy in Karamoja from 1898 to World War I was a policy of minimal interference, with what the British termed the "wilder tribes" inhabiting the large tract of the country to the north of Mount Elgon and between the Nile and Lake Rudolf.[25]

The policy of minimal interference meant two things. Karamoja District was destined to fall far behind in the development of educational, social, economic and government institutions which were being introduced in most parts of Uganda. Worst of all the policy did not mean freedom for the Karamojong. The Karamojong were to receive nothing new from the colonizers, other than those things they had to know and do in order to make British traders, adventurers and sportsmen prosper in Karamoja country. Karamoja was very famous for considerable numbers of elephants with unusual size tusks which roamed across its plains. The local people had always hunted elephants for meat, but had no use for the ivory. The first traders in Karamoja are said to have bought huge tusks of ivory for less than a handful of cheap beads. The British policy was not to interfere with the Karamojong as long as they provided enough labor for the colonial traders, adventurers and sportsmen. The Karamojong were also to stop their traditions which were disruptive of the white man's fun and exploitation of the Karamojong country.

The basis of Karamojong life and culture was and is cattle. Love for their cattle made the Karamojong fierce in the defense of their pastures as well as in raids against their neighbors for more cattle to increase their own herds. For the Karamojong, cattle constituted the principle form of saving, wealth, prestige, influence and numerous systems of gifts and debts. The pastoral values of the Karamojong were soon to be challenged by colonial policy that intended to make men available for manual labor for British adventurers.

Civil administration of Karamoja District started in 1921, with a district commissioner and an assistant district commissioner. The administration of the district had been responsible for ten ethnic groups within the area. The groups consisted of the Karamojong, the Dodoso, the Jie, the Nyakwai, the Upe, the Tepes, the Teusa, the Nyangea and the Poren. These groups, as most other ethnic groups in Uganda, had no common history or values to serve as a basis of unity. Nevertheless, the colonial framework grouped them together into one administrative unit divided into six counties, three of which were occupied by the Karamojong.

The extension of British political control over Karamoja meant that the Karamojong were to be ruled not by the elders but by the appointed chiefs, namely the district commissioners, county chiefs and their assistants. To make matters worse, the Karamojong were to be confined within a defined territory--something completely incompatible with the Karamojong way of life. At the end of Mr. Neville Dyson-Hudson's direct observation of the Karamojong in late 1958 he concluded that, "Karamojong adhere tenaciously to a scheme of pastoral values which leads them to pursue policies that are often at variance with those of government."[26]

Karamojong politics and social values, as already explained, were based on the politics and values of herding. The immediate major complaints against the government were government interference with cattle movements and its insistence on manual work. The pastoral life of the Karamojong was such that during the dry season the men were out with the herds, forty to eighty miles away from their permanent homes. To confine the movements of the Karamojong was to go against the main values of Karamojong society. Nevertheless, the British arbitrarily appointed chiefs who were expected to strictly confine cattle movements, in order that men were always available to provide porters, road gangs and food stuffs required of them by the colonial interests in the area.

> For the Karamojong life is governed by his herds. He is accustomed to making individual decisions about movements to particular areas for water and grazing. He is accustomed to the often lonely and always independent life of a herdsman. This is poor training for work in large organized groups. When government arrived he was forced to work as a porter carrying headloads, or as a laborer building government stations or clearing roads. The tribesmen did not like the new work and from the beginning the chiefs, who were the instruments used to raise the labour, were not popular.27

The appointed chiefs were bound to be unpopular for two major reasons. First, they had to carry out colonial orders which included restrictions to the extent that no Karamojong man would leave his permanent settlement without the knowledge and permission of the chief. The men had to be available whenever the colonialists wanted their labor. Secondly, the elders were and remained very influential leaders of public opinion in all Karamojong communities. They were absolutely opposed to the politics of appointed chiefs, and British policies that were incompatible with their way of life. In the Karamoja Annual Report of 1921, the influence of the elders was described as the greatest obstacle in the way of progress. According to the report, the majority of the appointed chiefs were mere puppets without authority and better men refused the position of chief because they feared the invincible influence of the elders.28

Nevertheless there were a few Karamojong who resolved to do the white man's bidding. Achia of Nabilatuk in the south of Karamoja was one of the chiefs described in 1923 by colonial officials as the brightest of the appointed chiefs in Karamoja District. After Mr. Lamb, the district commissioner, toured Achia's area, he wrote to his friend, Mr. Warner, the former district commissioner, that:

> At Achia's centre everything was very markedly satisfactory. I arrived in camp to find a large gathering, milk, water and fire wood in large quantities, also over sixty bowls of meal. . . . The porters who were to carry my loads on the following day were also ready awaiting me in camp. . . . The general condition of affairs is very good.29

Achia was young, intelligent and competent in the eyes of the colonial officials, because he had managed to carry out the district commissioner's orders. He permitted only half the men to be away at any one time to prevent everybody from disappearing to the grazing grounds, thereby leaving no work force for the government labor or crowds of people to welcome the touring colonial officials. Achia was good to the colonial officials but a tyrant to the Karamojong.

The elders met, discussed and called for the death of Achia in order that the people would be freed from forced labor and be able to herd their stock whenever they liked. The young men speared Achia to death and women came to dance and sing around Achia's body--rejoicing over the death of an enemy. Mr. Lamb returned to sentence three Karamojong to death and imprison others for Achia's murder.

It should be noted here that the Karamojong were resisting a government that demanded much from the people and gave nothing in return. The policy of non-interference was nothing more than the government taking freedom, labor and food for no tangible reward.

The Karamojong had every reason to hate the government and government agents. Hostility and resentment against the government as a whole was increased by the British policy of taxation which intended to force the Karamojong into selling their cattle to government buyers as an effort to overcome the shortage of meat for troops in East Africa during World War II. A poll-tax forced the Karamojong to part with hundreds of thousands of their cattle. Liebigs Ltd. alone is said to have bought cattle in Karamoja and exported them on an average of 8,000 cattle a year.[30] In short, the Karamojong colonial experience was one of conflict and sacrifice without rewards to the Karamojong.

The Karamojong traditional political system regarded killing of foreigners and raiding their neighbors for cattle appropriate and commendable. The government and its personnel were regarded as foreigners and at the same time troublemakers. The incompatibility of Karamojong values and colonial values was bound to lead to serious conflicts throughout the colonial period and also after independence.

> In recent years, heavy raiding has resulted in the introduction of large emergency police forces and detachments of the King's African Rifles until the disturbance is settled. There is thus awareness of the power of the government can muster when it chooses and of Karamojong inability to deal successfully with it. The pattern of behavior towards government is therefore less open conflict than simple disregard of its existence wherever possible, coupled with quiet breach of its policy where it conflicts with their own.[31]

To the Karamojong the government represents brutal force. The chiefs are to be feared and not respected for they are not backed by custom, age and the supernatural, but rather by force. According to most Karamojong, government and all its employees, regardless of origin or color, are a class of people which is difficult to deal with, which hates cattle and has no understanding of, or sympathy for, all-good pastoral values.

Toro Kingdom or District

Like Karamoja District, Toro Kingdom or District is a multi-ethnic group district. According to the 1959 census, the population of Toro District included:[32]

Ethnic Group	Population	Percentage
Baamba	32,866	9.4
Bakiga	5,824	1.7
Bakonjo	103,868	30.0
Banyankole	3,408	1.0
Banyarwanda	5,572	1.6
Banyoro	530	0.2
Batoro	183,492	52.4
Others	11,919	3.4
	347,479	99.3

The three major ethnic groups, namely, Batoro, Bakonjo and Baamba, had very different traditional political systems. Batoro had a centralized hierarchical political system very similar to that of Buganda and virtually identical with Bunyoro Kingdom from which they split in the nineteenth century. "The Batoro traditionally possessed a highly stratified social structure with the royal Bebito Clan (of Nilolic origin) on top, the pastoral cattle-keeping Bahims below them and the Bairi peasants at the bottom of the ladder."[33]

Unlike the Batoro, the Baamba and Bakonjo living on the slopes of the Ruwenzori Mountains as hunters and cultivators, were politically decentralized people. They organized their political systems on a level very similar to that of the Chiga, except that for the Baamba, the political unit was not an individual family but a village without a chief. The political system of the Baamba was "a relatively simple segmentary system based on shifting systems of alliances which depended upon the relationship of other villages to the village of the victim and of the aggressor."[34]

The villages made alliances to defend themselves from Bunyoro Kingdom and from the Batoro, who attempted to subjugate the Bakonjo and Baamba in order to collect tribute from them. Baamba and Bakonjo had for centuries managed to maintain their social and political independence from their neighbors. They also considered themselves civilized and free people compared to their neighbors in Batoro country and the Bunyoro Kingdom who lived under a highly stratified social structure.

Batoro country, a much smaller area than Toro District, came into existence as an independent political unit in 1830, when Prince Kaboyo rebelled against his father, the Omukama (king) of Bunyoro. Bunyoro Kingdom under Kabarega staged a series of attacks on Toro in the 1870's, which resulted in the reassertion of Bunyoro's control in 1889.

Kasagama, a Mutoro Prince and descendant of Kaboyo, made his escape to Buganda. With the assistance of Buganda and the British, he returned to Toro, drove Bunyoro out and restored his authority. Kasagama was reinstalled as Omukama of Toro in 1891. Kasagama was not only reinstalled as king of Toro country but also as king of all the people in what came to be called Toro Kingdom or District. As a result of this conflict, the resentment of Baganda in Bunyoro Kingdom increased, Toro and Bunyoro

Kingdom conflicts stopped but were not forgotten. The Toro Kingdom maintained a highly explosive internal political atmosphere throughout the colonial period. Baamba and Bakonjo resented and resisted Batoro political domination. "Chiefs dominated politics and administration in Toro until independence. A study of chiefship in the 1950's revealed that the royal clan provided few chiefs (12.5 per cent) of high or low rank, 45 per cent of the chiefs were sons of chiefs, while 40 per cent of the county chiefs were grandsons of the chiefs."[35]

This meant that almost all chiefs at the sub-county level and above were Batoro. Consequently, to most ethnic groups in Toro, all associations with colonial law, colonial policies, taxation and road gangs were associations inseparable from Batoro chiefs, who were the symbols and actual servants of the colonial government in the district. In addition to being ruled and dominated by Batoro, the Baamba and Bakonjo people resented Batoro as tax-collectors and the fact that their tax money was being used to support the royal family of Toro Kingdom. As a result, the talk about freedom and independence that was to sweep across Uganda was to mean in particular to the Baamba and Bakonjo, freedom from the Batoro. It was not surprising that during the independence period the Bakonjo and Baamba, failing to get a separate district within Uganda, resorted to declaring themselves an independent state. The Bakonjo and Baamba petitioned unsuccessfully to the United Nations Organization and the Organization of African Unity for membership.

What has been discussed so far gives ample knowledge of the political environment in Uganda in which the struggle for national unity and independence was about to be carried out. It is now safe and sound to say that the political history of an ethnic group in Uganda has been shaped by its respective geographical features and its traditional political, social and religious values.

British colonial policy forced the ethnic groups that had neither social nor administrative unity into a political union. The British not only ended their conflicts but also introduced numerous areas of actual or potentially serious conflicts between the ethnic groups.

The background so established will enable us to assess the presence of absence of a national consensus during and after the struggle for independence--the consensus that was to be a basis for a politically united and democratic Uganda.

3

National Consensus and the Struggle for National Unity

A recognition of ethnic group values and particularly the colonial experience of some ethnic groups is a prerequisite for an understanding of Uganda's political problems during her struggle for independence and national unity. Much time and space is being given to specific groups because their experiences are representative of other groups' experiences. Most important is the fact that with the understanding of the colonial experience of different groups, we can look at Uganda within the context of

Professor Truman's *Group Theory* to discover the underlying causes of what happened in Uganda before and after independence.

Professor David B. Truman, like many sociologists and psychologists, believes that man is in essence a social animal.[1] That is, every individual belongs to and is a participant in a number of groups which make up his social environment. According to Professor Truman, an individual's group affiliations, group experiences and the degree to which an individual identifies himself with his group or groups largely determine his attitudes, values and the frames of references in terms of which he interprets his experiences and perceives and evaluates events.[2]

The political behaviors and activities of the people of Uganda cannot be understood apart from the organized and potential groups in the political environment. We have already seen in Chapter 1 that ethnic groups were actual interest groups. Since the British effective control of Uganda in 1884-1886, the central government and its representatives became the final authoritative allocators of values in Uganda. Maintainence or enhancement of ethnic group values depended on the group's relationship with the colonial government. Buganda, like Batoro country, was able to acquire territory and entrench her control over her neighbors because of British support and approval. In a sense, ethnic groups had to gravitate toward the colonial government in order to protect or promote their values. This meant that the ethnic groups also functioned as political interest groups throughout the colonial era in that they made their claims through or upon the institutions of the colonial government.

This struggle for independence can, therefore, be viewed in terms of group political activities and ethnic group attitudes and values which were to be merged into a common endeavor for national independence.

Professor Truman gives two elements as the basis of unity and stability in any democratic political system. The elements are multiple or overlapping membership and the function of unorganized interest (potential) groups. Professor Truman maintains that the diversity of an individual's activities and attended interests involve him in a variety of actual and potential groups. Hence the individual finds himself holding many frames of reference resulting from many different groups in society. It is, therefore, from the overlapping membership and multiple loyalties that individuals come to share mutual interests.[3] The values shared in common become the basis for unity and disturbances in established relationships, and expectations anywhere in the society may produce new patterns of interaction aimed at restricting or eliminating the disturbance. In other words, in a society where there are common values, people may not be formally organized around those values, but when the values are threatened, they unite to defend those values. The values of interest groups and the values held in common by all people in society are, therefore, the basis for a national consensus.[4]

With this theory in mind, we can turn back to Uganda and look at the groups and the values that these groups held in common. There are some 28 ethnic groups of political significance in Uganda. Historically, these groups never had a need for unity. However, they did have much in common, but what they shared had never been significant enough in terms of bringing them together to induce mutual cooperation. Yet they were forcibly bundled into one political unit called Uganda and brought under British political and economic control with considerable participation in the colonization process by Baganda chiefs. The groups were joined together not as a result of any common values, but by aims contrary to most of the values of each group.

It should also be noted that as far as these groups are concerned, there are hardly any overlapping memberships and definitely no multiple loyalties to serve as a basis of unity. Keeping in mind the hostility and resentment between these groups (described earlier), one can rightly expect these groups to be actual and potential sources of disunity and instability, rather than sources of unity. The organized churches, labor unions, organized markets, Uganda Teachers Association, Uganda Bar Society, and a few other groups are in fact the only ones in Uganda that do cross the ethnic group boundaries. These groups crossing ethnic lines are examined in order to assess the presence or absence of a visible national consensus, during and after the struggle for independence.

The Uganda Bar Society includes members from many different ethnic groups within the country. However, less than half of the ethnic groups are represented. Like most other tightly organized groups in Uganda, the Bar Society is centered in Kampala, the capital of Uganda, and its membership is very small (perhaps no more than 200). In addition, the contacts of these members are so confined to the capital that their influence within their respective ethnic groups seems to disappear. Above all, as Professor Truman points out: "A measure of conformity to the norms of the group is the price of acceptance within it."[5] For example, a lawyer to command respect and acceptance by his own ethnic group is compelled to identify himself with the main ethnic group values and forms of traditional ways of acquiring positions of power. Those who do not conform to ethnic group values find themselves rejected in their own areas. A Muganda attempting to run for office in Bunyoro is like an ultra-liberal from New York trying to run for the U. S. Senate from the state of Georgia. A well-educated Karamojong who speaks highly of national law and order will inevitably find himself in situations similar to that of Achia (described earlier). As a result, the Bar Society does cross ethnic group boundaries and is a very important group for the country. But in terms of helping to achieve a national consensus, it is hardly significant.

The market system could have provided a basis for free contact between different peoples of Uganda. Colonial policies, however, were such that Africans were given very little chance to do business.

> In Uganda, official policy towards the marketing of native crops and general trade has been extremely restrictive since almost the beginning of British administration. . . . As early as 1901 the Uganda government was displaying a passion for tidiness and a distaste for petty traders. The government zoning legislation and the Produce Marketing Ordinance of 1933, consolidated a rigid framework into which it was virtually impossible for small scale African entrepreneurs to penetrate.[6]

What this meant in political terms was that the colonial market system did not in any significant way increase group interaction.

As a result of taxation, the Karamojong were forced to part with some of their cattle usually with government agents there to do the buying. In other parts of Uganda people were compelled to grow cotton and coffee but the buying was done by Asians. The economic conditions made the Africans economically dependent on Britain. Britain set the price and the amount of cotton to be produced, therefore the different groups in the country never had to feel a need for each other.

The organized churches are potentially important aspects of Uganda's political system, but so far they have proved politically impotent when faced with ethnic group loyalties. In other words, a Munyoro Roma-Catholic can identify himself with a Muganda Roman Catholic, but once there is conflict between Bunyoro and Buganda, a Muganda Roman Catholic is no better or worse off than a Muganda Muslem in the eyes of a Munyoro Roman Catholic. Probably the most interesting and best example of the insignificance of organized churches in Ugandan politics is the experience of the Democratic party in the Buganda Kingdom.

Since the succession wars or religious civil wars in Buganda, Protestants have had a monopoly over certain top government posts in Buganda.

> Inconceivably British colonial officials soon became entangled in the dispute and were forced to take sides. As it happened, they gave their support to the Protestant party, led by the chief minister (Katikiro) of the kingdom, Apolo Kagwa, initially the smallest of the factions fighting in the war, but the one enjoying the confidence of the Anglican mission. This support was crucial for Katikiro Kagwa.[7]

Kagwa's party won, and soon afterwards Apolo Kagwa was to sign the 1900 Uganda Agreement with the British representative, Mr. Johnson.

> The agreement ensured the ascendancy of Kagwa's party within the Buganda political system in four important ways. First it marked the political victory within Buganda of Kagwa's kind of Christianity. Hence-forward as D. A. Low has commented election to chiefly office within that kingdom was to be disposed according to affiliations

which were heavily weighted in favor of Kagwa's faction.8

Since 1900, a few Catholics and Muslems have held important offices. Over 80 per cent of the posts of power in Buganda have been in the hands of Protestants in spite of the fact that in Buganda, about 50 per cent of the people were Catholics. There were more Catholics than Protestants in Buganda. Nevertheless the Kabaka and prime minister as a rule were Anglicans as was true of the majority of Saza and Gombolola chieftaincies until the Obote Revolution of 1966. As a result of political domination it was mainly the Protestants who enjoyed most of the economic benefits resulting from land reforms and systems of self-paid chiefs within Buganda and outside of Buganda. It has always been common talk in Buganda that if one wished to be a chief or had hopes of getting a bursary or foreign scholarship from the Buganda government, one should profess Anglicanism.

Unquestionably, Buganda has had a history of conflicts fought on a religious basis. It was in Buganda that one would expect to find organized churches as viable political forces commanding the loyalty of the people. In Buganda there have been many well-educated and competent Roman Catholics denied top paying jobs and denied scholarships on the grounds that they were Catholics. It was these victims of a political system based on religious affiliations who stood firmly for elected officials rather than representation by appointment. The Democratic party, led by a lawyer and staunch Roman Catholic, Mr. Kiwanuka, did not hesitate to make known these grievances of the Catholics in Buganda. The

Catholic Church's Archbishop of Uganda, Dr. Kiwanuka, in 1961, wrote a pastoral letter defining the roles of political parties, free and fair elections and constitutional monarchy.[9] The letter was sent to all parishes. It contained nothing against traditional authority. It just amounted to giving complete support for the drive for a popularly and freely elected government in Buganda as well as in the rest of Uganda.

The Kabaka of Buganda and his Protestant chiefs were angered by the archbishop's message for they were opposed to any form of direct election. To show their displeasure and power, they ordered the arrest of the archbishop. His Grace, Archbishop Joseph Kiwanuka was out of the country, so it was his assistant, Monseigneur Sbayigga, that was arrested and detained for a token hour on November 23, 1961. It was at this point that I remember becoming almost certain that Mr. Benedict Kiwanuka and his political party (the Democratic party) would carry Buganda in the pending elections. The elections before and after this episode demonstrated the Kabaka's hold over the people of Buganda Kingdom. The Kabaka's government sent out messages through chiefs that the people of Buganda should not vote. According to *Africa Report* of October, 1964, less than 3 per cent of eligible voters voted in Buganda in the 1961 March elections.

Hardly a year later and a few months after the archbishop incident, the Kabaka and Buganda government realized that elected government was the only way to independence. They approved and endorsed elections after forming their own party--Kabaka Yekka which means "king only." In the election of February, 1962, over 95 per cent of eligible voters in Buganda cast their votes and Kabaka Yekka emerged victorious with an overwhelming majority. Kabaka Yekka won 65 seats and only three seats were won by the Democratic party (DP) in the 68 elected seats of Buganda Lukiiko. Actually, the three DP members won in the "Lost Counties" where 70 per cent to 80 per cent of the people are of the Bunyoro Kingdom but lived under Buganda rule as a result of the 1900 Agreement. Their vote represented a vote against Buganda domination.

A. K. Mayanja, a Muslim Muganda, lawyer and then minister of education in Buganda government described the elections in the following terms:

> One of the brightest features of the Kabaka Yekka victory is that it dealt what I should like to think was a fatal blow at the ugly head of religion in politics. Until the Kabaka Yekka victory, even a person as normally reasonable as myself used to regard every Roman Catholic as a member of the Democratic party or a DP sympathizer until he proved the contrary. The Roman Catholic church entered the Lukiiko election with a zeal and a relish and a determination which left most of us really aghast. But as the poll showed, most Roman Catholics, including by the way, a few nuns and priests, voted Kabaka Yekka and not for the Democratic party.[10]

It is worth noting that DP candidates did not win in counties like Buddu where Catholics are more than 70 per cent of the electorate. I am of the conviction since those elections that loyalty of people to their ethnic groups and their traditional leaders is so powerful a force that other inlfuences in conflict with it are practically impotent.

Trade and Labor Unions

Trade and labor unions can be powerful and dynamic factors, which on the political, economic and social planes might cross ethnic group lines and might contribute toward consensus in society. Unfortunately, in Uganda trade and labor unions never developed to points where they could exert considerable influence on social, economic, or political life. Organized labor played an active part in Uganda's struggle against colonial domination, but their influence in terms of a national consensus was practically insignificant. Uganda did well as a cash crop peasantry economy as early as 1930, thus making it unnecessary to introduce a plantation economy in the country. As a result most Africans have always been self-employed, making the membership of organized labor too small for its impact to be effective. Uganda's pay work-force did not exceed 300,000 out of a population of 10 millions (1970 estimates). The labor forces not only remained a very tiny portion of the population, but also its members were located almost exclusively in the urban and industrial areas of Kampala, the national capital. Kampala, being the center of government, commerce, education and most employment, was a vital center of communication. Nevertheless, Kampala, being located in the heart of Buganda Kingdom, was the worst place for political activism. Buganda allowed little room for political activism. The colonial officials, too, did not hesitate to discourage national trade union endeavors for they knew that such programs would inevitably hasten and strengthen the local challenge to colonial rule. The restrictive colonial policies towards union activities, the instability of union leadership, the small size of their number, the concentration of their administrative activities in Kampala, their lack of funds and experienced leadership did not allow the unions and their leaders to contribute significantly to any form of national consensus.

In summary, one might well come to the conclusion that there were no values held in common by all Baganda, other than the common desire for independence from British control. The lack of multiple loyalties and multiple memberships made Uganda void of common aims, common points of reference and common goals which could serve as a national consensus.

Political Parties

The real attempt to create a national consensus did not come until the formation of political parties; as a result of a lack of common values and attitudes, the development of national parties was soon to prove a formidable task.

As early as 1950, a few Ugandan educated elite had a great awareness of the

Dr. Obote meeting with Harold Wilson, British Prime Minister, in London. (Courtesy of British Information Services)

Bulange: Headquarters of the Kabaka's Government.

A Kabaka of Buganda reviews his troops.

Political meeting in Uganda.

need and importance for creating national unity during and after the struggle for independence. As a result of this feeling E. M.K. Mulira, a Muganda teacher and journalist founded the Uganda National Congress in 1952. From its early days the Uganda National Congress tried to establish itself and maintain itself as a national political party. The emphasis of the party was the common need, desire and longing for independence. The party, for some obvious reasons, had little chance to succeed. It was the first political group in Uganda, organized on basis other than ethnicity.

> As for the Europeans, there has never been a specifically European political organization in Uganda. If the Governor of Uganda wished to address himself specifically to the European community, almost the only opportunity available to him was the annual dinner of the Caledonian Society. Other expatriate groups in Uganda . . . have also had their tribal societies but none of these organizations, European, African, or indeed the various Asian communal organizations either, were ever in any significant sense political. They certainly never provided anything for African politicains to copy.[11]

As late as 1952, political parties and party politics were completely new in Uganda. The absence of a lingua franca in Uganda and the vested interests in ethnic group political organizations presented the Uganda National Congress with formidable problems in its attempts to operate on a national basis. Furthermore, its headquarters were in Kampala, the capital of Uganda, but located in Buganda; and its leaders were Baganda. For people outside Buganda the party represented a revival of the Buganda political domination of 1894-1930. Uganda National Congress not only failed outside Buganda, but also failed to command respect and support in Buganda, for after all, as a political party it stood for a revolutionary way of acquiring power. For instance, in 1960 the prime minister of the Buganda Kingdom wrote on its behalf:

> From time immemorial the Baganda have known no other ruler above their Kabaka in his kingdom, and still they do not recognize any other person whose authority does not derive from the Kabaka and is exercised on his behalf.[12]

In Buganda all power was derived from the Kabaka. The idea of deriving power from political parties was, therefore, not only undesirable but dangerous in the eyes of the majority of Baganda. It was not until the Kabaka formed his own party, "Kabaka Yekka," in 1961, that the overwhelming majority of Baganda became willing to participate in elections. The experience of Uganda National Congress was something from which other leaders had to draw their lessons. The people in Buganda were not willing to accept authority other than that from the Kabaka. Although Uganda National Congress failed, the party should remain an integral part of the political history of Uganda. It was this party that laid the foundation for the Uganda Peoples Congress--the party that ruled Uganda from independence in 1962 to the day of the military take-over on January 25th, 1971.

In spite of the absence of a common national consensus and the presence of deep-rooted devisive ethnic group loyalties, the nationalists (like Dr. Milton Obote and Ben Kiwanuka) continued their drive to get around the immovable ethnic group loyalties and to build some form of unity that could bring Uganda to independence.

The great issue of self-determination (independence) was not a strong enough basis upon which to cultivate dynamic nationalism. The leaders of the Uganda Peoples Congress and the leaders of the Democratic party therefore found themselves confronted with the great problem of creating party propaganda which could build up, among the largest sector possible of the population, an attitude of loyalty, commitment and enthusiasm for national goals rather than ethnic group goals.

What Dr. Nkrumah observed in West African politics applies equally as well to the peoples of Uganda. He concluded that, "We must remember that educational backwardness of colonial countries, the majority of the people in the country cannot read. There is only one thing they can understand and that is 'action.'"[13] In other words, political speeches in terms of political, social and economic ideologies meant very little, if anything, to the masses.

It was, therefore, not only advisable but essential that nationalist elites should use the language and ideas that the illiterate and semi-literate could understand. But most unfortunately, it was almost impossible to talk their language without offending their ethnic group loyalties. In many areas even the local issues like water supplies, roads, schools and clinics could not be easily utilized to arouse the enthusiasm of the masses. For instance, in Buganda, as in most kingdoms, roads, schools and clinics were services people thought to be entirely provided by local governments. And as such, an exposure of the inadequacies of these services and promise for better services seemed in most cases to be a reflection of sentiments against traditional rule and lack of respect for those in the local governments (the king and his chiefs). In Buganda, for example, the promise of more primary schools and secondary schools by the Democratic party was considered an attempt to out-do the Kabaka. Therefore, Benedict Kiwanuka, as president of the Democratic party, was considered a traitor to the Baganda. Kiwanuka's ability to secure foreign scholarship was also equally resented by both the Buganda government and majority of the masses. It was unthinkable to most Baganda that an ordinary man like Kiwanuka could provide the services through his party--services which for decades were considered gifts from the Kabaka of Buganda. Under these circumstances, it seems as if Kiwanuka was trying to undermine the responsibilities of the Kabaka.

The political party leaders tried to employ all that was shared in common to mobilize the masses. But whatever method they chose, they found themselves in conflict with local sentiments and values. In Buganda for instance, the Democratic party tried to employ communal activities as part of the propaganda. Traditional ceremonies such as singing, groups of drummers following the party leaders, ethnic group dances in the party leaders' honor, communally-built shelters and platforms, decorations for political rallies, ethnic group musicians, free beer parties and food contributions toward group cooking and feasting at political party meetings were ways in which to involve the masses. Such activities were considered privileges for the Kabaka, princes of Buganda and the Kabaka's important chiefs.

From personal experience (1960-1965) I know that full participation in these activities meant change or shift of loyalty and betrayal of traditional authority. To most Baganda, full participation in political party activities was an outright fundamental conflict of loyalty that a citizen owed to the Kabaka and an affront to the Kabaka himself. As a result of these unfortunate feelings, most Democratic party leaders and staunch members found themselves in precarious circumstances. Many were beaten up, houses were burned and sometimes crops, such as bananas, sugar cane and coffee trees, were razed by the pangas and axes of those who felt it was their duty to show their indignation of party politics and to demonstrate their solidarity with the Kabaka. Party politics were doomed in Buganda unless based on traditional political values where all authority had to be acquired from the Kabaka and exercised on the Kabaka's behalf.

In other parts of Uganda, as in Buganda, party politics were faced with insurmountable problems. In Karamoja, for instance, government and national politics were objects of resentment and instruments of oppression and exploitation. Some

African politicians were, to all intents and purposes, scared of the implications of freedom and independence. For the Karamojong, freedom and independence meant freedom to raid outside societies for cattle--a movement that had been practically stopped by colonial policy. Freedom and independence implied restoration of one-sixth Karamojong country alienated by Pokot between 1900-1930 with actual and obvious government approval.

After direct observation of the Karamojong from January 1956 to September 1958, Neville Dyson-Hudson stated that:

> Karamojong political world, covers both Europeans and natives of any origin employed by administration. As far as Karamojong are concerned, the general features of persons in this class are that 'they are difficult' and that 'they eat cattle'-- that is government has no understanding of or sympathy for, their pastoral values and thus no appreciation of the steps necessary to safeguard them.[14]

In Karamoja, as elsewhere in Uganda, the Nationalists were the educated and one time employees of the government. Their task was not only to shout "independence" but to cry "independence" in terms that could be understood and thus generate support. But there was no way they could come out with definitions of independence that could be acceptable to their own people, as well as their neighboring ethnic groups. For instance, if one shouted that the elders should rule and police stations should be demolished, one would expect Karamojong support but only at the expense of possible support from the neighboring peoples who for centuries had tasted the bitter contacts with the Karamojong in the process of cattle raiding.

The prospects of independence flared up the Bunyoro-Buganda conflict over the "Lost Counties." According to Bunyoro Kingdom, political independence among other things meant "justice." The British must go and the "Lost Counties" returned became the theme for independence in Bunyoro. Meanwhile, chiefs in Buganda were publicly declaring that the so-called disputed counties were an integral part of Buganda. Early in 1962, I attended a meeting at Mpigi (a small town in Buganda) where one of the Kabaka's most important chiefs declared that "as far as our counties are concerned--absolutely no negotiation. They were acquired through bloodshed and can only be taken away through bloodshed. If Banyoro wants--they can fight." This one issue made party politics almost impossible. To have support in Buganda, one had got to identify himself with the Kabaka. Actually, one had to be a Kabaka's man, which meant that support in Buganda meant no support at all in the Bunyoro Kingdom, for no Kabaka's man could dare endorse the alienation of the Kabaka's territory.

Toro Kingdom was another interesting case where problems were mainly internal. The Baamba-Bakonjo were more than determined to fight Batoro political domination. They viewed independence not so much in terms of British control but Batoro control. Like in Buganda, to have Batoro support, one had to be on good terms with the king of Toro. To be supported by Batoro, therefore, meant automatic loss of Baamba-Bakonjo support (meaning 40 per cent of the votes of Toro Kingdom) (see population figures on page 71). Baamba and Bakonjo were resolved to form a district of their own completely independent of Toro Kingdom. The Batoro, like Baganda on the "Lost Counties," were not prepared to part with an inch of their territory. The issue was unresolvable and no compromise seemed possible. The Baamba-Bakonjo demand for a separate district had more than local impact. A politician who dared hint on the possibility of an independent Baamba-Bakonjo district would not only lose the Batoro vote but also find himself in deep waters in Buganda where the "Lost Counties" issues was uncompromisable.

It was in this unquestionably consensusless political environment of Uganda, with unresolvable, enduring conflicts of political power, land and values, that party politics were going to mobilize the masses in the drive for national independence. Independence with or without national unity was the fundamental basis for common action against British rule.

4

The Politics of Independence

The ethnic group political behavior and attitudes had made it clear to some nationalists that inter-party politics and party politics were the only way for national progress towards independence. The nationalists (like Dr. Obote, Mr. Benedict Kiwanuka, Abu Mayanja, Mulira, etc.) realized a need for national unity as early as 1950, but their attempts to organize a national mass movement failed until the crisis of 1953-1955. The colonial secretary's speech, reported in the East African Standard of July 3, 1953, referred to the possibility of an East African Federation. Buganda was alarmed by the suggested federation of East Africa. The immediate reaction of the Kabaka and the Great Lukiiko was a demand for the immediate transfer of Buganda from the colonial office to the foreign office and the setting of a time limit for the declaration of the independence of Buganda. The Federation of East Africa was completely unacceptable to Buganda on the grounds that the Kabaka and his power would decline within a larger union; that the special position of Buganda in Uganda would be threatened; and that the Baganda had every reason to believe that the federated territories of Kenya, Uganda and Tanzania would inevitably come under the domination of the white minority in Kenya.

As a result of Buganda's strong and intensive negative reaction to the federation, as well as the negative reactions from most parts of East Africa, the idea of a federated East Africa was immediately abandoned. Unfortunately, the governor of Uganda's attempts to reassure the Kabaka and his ministers that federation would not be imposed on Uganda did not prove convincing.

> Buganda grew increasingly alarmed and suspicious and after protracted interviews between the Kabaka and the governor, the former refused to recommend to his Great Lukiiko the Protectorate government's proposals for a new constitution for a United Uganda, with a legislative assembly to which the Great Lukiiko should appoint representatives.[1]

Apparently the Kabaka had already made a decision. He was not only opposed to East African federation but also viewed a creation of a united Uganda as a step towards the federation. In addition, without the Kabaka's recommendation, any new constitution was doomed. Buganda was to stand firm for Buganda's independence as a sovereign state. As a consequence of the Kabaka's refusal to cooperate with the governor, the protectorate government withdrew its recognition of the Kabaka and his authority. But the Kabaka's authority existed strictly and completely between the Baganda and their Kabaka. Knowing that it could neither dethrone nor curb the Kabaka's authority without violence, the protectorate government deported the Kabaka to England on November 30, 1953.

The news of the Kabaka's forced departure stunned all Baganda. The sense of shock in Buganda is well described in "The King's Men."

> Work was at an end; people stood in knots at road junctions mostly silently and staring; women sat at their house doors weeping. Girl interviewers employed by the East African Institute of Social Research spoiled their questionnaires by the tears that fell on them and they had to be let off work. Educated men were angry, and even previous critics of the Kabaka were violent in their denunciation of the protectorate government.[2]

The exile of the Kabaka created a new sense of unity in Buganda. Buganda nationalism and the Kabaka were one and the Kabaka was universally spoken of as the sovereign to whom all Baganda owed allegiance. At this point, the masses in Buganda seemed ready for mobilization into mass movements. The Uganda National Congress (UNC), formed in 1952, was vocal in its denunciations of the British government action and in December, 1953, organized a deputation to London to protest the Kabaka's exile. The UNC gained support in Buganda, but the Kabaka's subsequent return in November, 1955, did not help the party. It only strengthened and consolidated unity and oneness of the Baganda behind the Kabaka.

The Kabaka's exile led to the Agreement of 1955, by which Buganda practically achieved internal self-government at the expense of her demand for sovereignty and territorial integrity. Through the agreement the Kabaka had agreed to have Buganda represented on the Legislative Council of Uganda, the issue on which the Kabaka had been deported. The agreement also transformed the traditional Kabakaship into a constitutional monarchy and introduced elected offices in Buganda. The chief minister of Buganda was to be elected by the Great Lukiiko. Another five ministers were to be selected by the chief minister from a list of fifteen chosen by the Lukiiko. The agreement also called for direct election to the Great Lukiiko which was to be composed of a maximum of ninety-three members, including a speaker, six ministers, six personal nominees of the Kabaka, twenty county chiefs and sixty representative members. In short, the Agreement of 1955 and Kabaka's exile made it clear that Buganda would remain an integral part of Uganda. The agreement also was a giant step towards the democratization of politics in Buganda in terms of elected and representative officials.

Signing the Agreement of 1955 was the condition for the Kabaka's return and a foundation for the constitutional developments which were to turn the Uganda protectorate into an independent state. In the eyes of most of Baganda, however, the agreement was nothing more than a dead letter. The Kabaka's return was overwhelmingly viewed as a complete victory of the Kabaka over the governor of Uganda and the British government. The victor-vanquished relationship was widely accepted and supportive examples were simple but convincing. For instance, the fact that the governor had poured tea for the Kabaka at the governor's garden party was circulated and emphasized in most Buganda papers. In Buganda pouring drinks is a duty of young people, people lower in rank, servants or pages. The governor's action was therefore widely interpreted as a demonstration of the servant-master relationship between the governor and the lion of Buganda.

As a matter of fact, it was common gossip in my home and school area that while in exile the Kabaka was hosted in Buckingham Palace, where he was seduced by Queen Elizabeth II but had refused her.

In any case, practically all Baganda, except a few highly educated ones who knew the implications of the 1955 Agreement, viewed the Kabaka as the all powerful king who was returning to resume all the powers of his great grandfather, Mutesa I.

"Mutesa I invited the Europeans into Buganda and Mutesa II was going to order the Europeans out of Buganda," according to the most sincere beliefs of most Baganda. The Kabaka's duties in the eyes of Baganda, as described in *Gabunga*, a Luganda newspaper were:

1. To sack all traitors (governor included).

2. To fix cotton and coffee prices in the peasants' interests.

3. To govern as his forefathers did.

4. To change the newly signed 1955 Agreement in which he had agreed to a united Uganda and the change of his status to a constitutional monarchy.[3]

All in all the deportation and the 1955 Agreement strengthened rather than weakened the Kabaka's formidable hold on the peoples of Buganda.

Even to most educated Baganda, "constitutional monarchy" was neither understood nor regarded seriously. To them, the agreement was signed to prevent further conflict between the British officials and the Kabaka--conflicts which could possibly result in the second deportation and more bloodshed in Buganda. Most important was the Kabaka's hold on the peasantry. "The bulk of the population did not want any limitation of the royal powers. In fact, since their king was the national hero and battering ram in the fight for an independent status, they wanted to increase the

Kabaka's right and privileges rather than to control them."[4]

The Kabaka's return, the celebrations for his return and his tour of Buganda immediately afterwards made the Kabaka a formidable force in the politics of independence and intensified Baganda's desire to see British authority removed. The following seven years (1955-1962) were to see the actual struggle for national independence. In the seven years three commissions and two constitutional conferences took place.

The conferences dealt with the issues of Buganda's special position in Uganda, the position of the other kingdoms, the different attitudes of the peoples of Uganda, the "Lost Counties" and the Baamba-Bakonjo drive for an independent district. In spite of these issues, however, it was clear that no political party was capable of mobilizing mass support independent of the traditional leaders. Support in Buganda was viewed as crucial but impossible to achieve without the Kabaka's approval.

In search of massive support and as an attempt of minimizing conflicts of loyalty between national goals and ethnic group leadership, political parties had no alternative but to try to draw the traditional leaders whose influences were strong in the localities into the leadership of major party branches, district and regional committees. Political parties found themselves also obligated to make certain local alliances with traditional leaders, hence bringing into party leadership people whose mentality and goals were ethnic, regional or religious or a combination of the three. The central leadership of the parties was national in outlook and to a reasonable extent denounced clan, religious, ethnic group and regional politics. The parties as a whole remained loose alliances of traditional elements with nationalist politicians whose common interest was the removal of British authority.

Association of a political party with traditional authority in an area meant immediate mass support for the party, but at the expense of national unity. Most traditional leaders were regional-minded and as such endangered party unity on a national level. The most important fact was that alliances with traditional leaders were within themselves a threat to national unity. The uneasy alliance between Uganda Peoples Congress and Kabaka Yekka,[5] for instance, meant an automatic loss of support for UPC in Bunyoro. For Bunyoro, an alliance with the Kabaka meant commitment on Obote's part that the "Lost Counties" were an integral part of Buganda Kingdom. As a result of the UPC and KY alliance, UPC did not win a single national parliamentary seat for Bunyoro Kingdom in the 1962 national election.

In Toro Kingdom, like in Buganda, it was essential for one to have an informal or formal alliance with the Mukama (king) in order to have Batoro support. However, being on good terms with the Mukama meant near automatic loss of support of Baamba-Bakonjo since such ties meant that one supported the Batoro political domination in the Baamba and Bakonjo country. In Karamoja, as already observed, to be on acceptable political terms was to demonstrate complete commitment to Karamojong values, but such commitment would not only mean abolition of national government but also automatic loss of support of the peoples who had had experience with Karamojong raids for cattle. Buganda in particular stood out as the real threat to national unity. "The protracted and difficult negotiations over the new constitution were largely caused by the passionate struggle of Buganda to reach the special position she was determined to have in the new Uganda."[6]

The new constitution was the 1962 document that brought Uganda to independence. During these negotiations, Mutesa II, the Kabaka of Buganda, took a leading part in all major negotiations with the British and the protectorate governments. The British regarded the Kabaka as the symbolic head because of the 1955 Agreement, but the people of the Buganda Kingdom were, as their ancestors, viewing the Kabaka as a traditional monarch with executive authority who rules rather than merely reigning. The British believed that the 1955 Agreement made the Kabaka an adviser to his ministers and the Great Lukiiko, but in fact the Kabaka was in an unquestionable position to control the actions of both the Lukiiko and ministers in Buganda.

Mutesa II was present in London throughout the two constitutional conferences, the outcome of which was the national constitution which gave Buganda the power to elect indirectly, by the Great Lukiiko, her representative to the National Assembly. The concession to Buganda's demand for indirect election of her representative to the National Assembly made the Kabaka indispensable in anyone's attempt to secure a Buganda parliamentary seat in the National Assembly.

By 1960 Buganda Kingdom had failed to win her demands for federal status in an independent Uganda. The British government had also denied Buganda's demand to:

- a) Have a Buganda army and freedom to make her own military alliance with other countries, particularly Britain.

- b) Have all present Ugandan police forces responsible for the Buganda province automatically come under Buganda government's jurisdiction at independence.

- c) Have an independent Buganda high court and district courts. Buganda High Court was to be on an equal basis as the National High Court and appeals from it would only be to the East African Court of Appeal and finally to the Privy Council.

- d) Have commerce and industry located in Buganda to be licensed in Buganda and all excise duty to go to the Buganda Kingdom treasury.

- e) Have all existing institutions of learning located in Buganda, except Makerere University College to fall under the jurisdiction of Buganda government.

Failing to achieve all these demands, Buganda made an abortive attempt to secede from Uganda. On December 30, 1960, the Buganda Parliament passed and announced a resolution declaring that in the name of God and the Nation of Buganda, British protection in Buganda was at an end as from midnight of December 31, 1960.

The British persuaded and militarily threatened the Baganda out of their determination to be a separate autonomous state, with or without the approval of Her Majesty's government. When the secession move failed the Buganda government declared a boycott of the first countrywide direct election to the legislative council in March, 1961. The Democratic party and the Uganda Peoples Congress campaigned for the elections notwithstanding the Kabaka's apparent approval of the election boycott in Buganda.

> The election was held on schedule in March, 1961, but only three percent of the eligible voters in Buganda went to the polls and their fluke vote gave the Democratic party 20 of the 21 Buganda elected seats in the Central Legislative Council.[7]

In spite of the successful boycott of election in Buganda, the protectorate government recognized the Democratic party's victory over Uganda Peoples Congress, and Mr. Benedict Kiwanuka, the president of the Democratic party, became chief minister when Britain gave Uganda internal self-government in May, 1961. The Democratic party's victory and Kiwanuka's new position of power in the National Assembly was widely understood as a direct affront to the Kabaka, for he had through his chiefs ordered a boycott of the elections.

Consequently, Kiwanuka and all those who had voted were branded as traitors to Buganda's cause and a threat to the throne. Worse still was the fact that Kiwanuka was a Catholic, and no Catholic had held top office in Buganda since the Protestant victory of 1892 described earlier. But Kiwanuka's victory had made it absolutely clear that inter-party politics in Buganda was inevitable.

As a reaction to the Democratic party victory and pending Kiwanuka's new role as chief minister, the predominantly Protestant land owners and notables in Buganda met and decided to start a mass movement for the purpose of ousting the Democratic party and Benedict Kiwanuka and asserting Buganda's identity and the Kabaka's power in the approaching independence. The outcome of the meeting was that Kabaka Yekka, which was hailed by its founders as the Baganda movement that would safeguard the Kabakaship.

Membership to Kabaka Yekka (KY) was the pledge in itself to show loyalty to the throne and solidarity to ensure that political change would not destroy Buganda's heritage. Membership was also considered as an oath that the Kabaka had always been and was going to remain the only ruler of Buganda.

The KY appeals focused on the Kabakaship were certain to arouse immediate massive support from the populace which had already been particularly devoted to the throne and all it represents since the 1953-1955 crisis.

Kabaka Yekka's election symbol was
a chair, strongly reminiscent of the
throne, and no other policy objectives
beyond protection of the throne were
presented to the voters. The most
effective piece of campaign propaganda was a booklet called *Kabaka
Atte Nabbe* (The Kabaka Against the
Enemy), in which a graphic pictorial
comparison was made of the kind of
government that the Baganda could
expect from the Democratic party
(with the Kabaka at the bottom of
the ladder of power) and from Kabaka
Yekka (with the Kabaka at the top).
Although the Kabaka Yekka leadership
denied authorship of the booklet, it
was known as the "KY manifesto" in
the rural areas. Because Democratic
party supporters were virtually the
only Baganda who had dared to participate in the 1961 elections, they
were everywhere attacked as the arch
enemies of the Kabaka and of Buganda.
This attack had strong religious
overtones, thus perpetuating the
traditional religious cleavage that
has always characterized politics
in Buganda.[8]

With such propaganda, a victory was imminent and in the February, 1962, Buganda
legislative election, the Democratic party
suffered a crushing defeat in Buganda.
Kabaka Yekka won 65 of the 68 seats. The
three that the Democratic party candidates
did elect were chosen from the "Lost Counties" where the Banyoro outnumber the Baganda and anti-Baganda feeling was strong.
It is widely believed in Buganda that the
Kabaka personally approved each name of
the KY candidate who was to stand for the

direct elections to the Buganda Lukiiko. Since it was the duty of the Lukiiko to appoint Buganda's twenty-one representatives to the National Assembly, it was clear that for a political party to have a majority in the assembly it would need personal approval of the Kabaka.

In the April 1962 elections in all parts of Uganda except Buganda Kingdom, UPC had won 37 seats and DP had won 24 seats. The Kabaka's men appointed by the Lukiiko to represent Buganda in the National Parliament were to decide the national leadership that would lead Uganda to independence. Total elected seats were 82 and Buganda Lukiiko had 21 of them to give away at will. It was with this Kabaka Yekka, a purely ethnic group party, that Dr. Milton Obote's Uganda Peoples Congress had to make an uneasy alliance which led to a coalition central government under which Uganda became independent on October 9, 1962.

Dr. Obote's timing was very important. The parliamentary election outside of Buganda was held in April, 1962, and in May, 1962, KY's alliance with the UPC enabled Obote to win the majority seats in Parliament. The alliance with Kabaka Yekka brought the UPC and Obote to power but at considerable cost in terms of national unity and good-will. Kabaka Yekka propaganda had already declared that no man can be "above" the Kabaka on Buganda soil-- "above" meaning in prestige and political power. In order to prepare the way for the alliance, Obote had also agreed with the Kabaka's demands in the London conference for an independent High Court of Buganda whose decisions were to be as final as the decisions of the National High Court. Obote had also supported Buganda's demand for full federal status within Uganda. Above all, it was common belief and common gossip throughout Buganda that part of the agreement between Obote and the Kabaka was that the Kabaka was to be the head of state in Uganda. All in all, most Baganda sincerely believed that the Kabaka as a constitutional monarch and head of state was to have more power than the autocratic powers of the governor, for the Kabaka was the founder of justice and he received no orders, as the governor did from the colonial office.

On the whole the widely held attitudes and beliefs in Buganda, plus the facts that Buganda had won herself a privileged political and economic position within Uganda, the KY-UPC alliance came to mean Buganda Kingdom's first sure step toward the resumption of Buganda's political domination of 1900-1930.

Noting that Uganda achieved her independence with Dr. Obote's Uganda Peoples Congress in alliance with Kabaka Yekka and that throughout Uganda there was nothing that one can refer to as a national consensus, one can only come to the conclusion that at Independence Day, October 9, 1962, Uganda was nothing more than a "paper nation." Independence Day was an end of British authority in Uganda and a beginning of a new era, an era for the Ugandan nationalists who had the very difficult task of maintaining the state of Uganda and toiling for the creation of one nation out of the self-centered exclusive ethnic groups of Uganda.

5

The Post-Independence Politics and the Obote Revolution

The years following independence were bound to be years of drastic political change in Uganda. Dr. Obote's Uganda Peoples Congress in alliance with Kabaka Yekka had firmly placed Obote into actual political power on Independence Day, October 9, 1962. Nevertheless, most Baganda believed that Buganda Kingdom would not be ruled by the central government. It appeared as if Buganda and the Kabaka would be the informal but also the effective leaders of Ugandan politics.

The UPC alliance with Kabaka Yekka was in itself a source of serious concern outside Buganda.

> Concern for the status of their rulers and fear of domination by the Buganda has clearly increased in recent months in the western province as a result of the UPC alliance with Kabaka Yekka. In other parts of Uganda, too, the one question that assumed UPC alliance with Kabaka Yekka and the implications of this alliance for the central government.[1]

Matters were not improved when Democratic party candidates outside of Buganda decided to use the KY-UPC alliance as a political issue. The candidates did not hesitate to state or imply that Obote had "sold the country" to the Kabaka of Buganda. "DP speakers pointed out that the Buganda representatives in the National Assembly, indirectly and undemocratically elected by the Lukiiko, would be at the beck and call of that body and unable therefore to think in terms of the country as a whole. The result, they argued, would be the domination of the central government by Buganda."[2]

The Democratic party candidates running for offices in the by-election for Toro's two seats in Parliament on May 2, 1962, expanded on these fears by suggesting that economic development in their respective areas would inevitably suffer as a direct result of the UPC alliance with Kabaka Yekka, since the prominent leaders of Buganda's abortive secession move in 1960 were the leaders of Kabaka Yekka, a party that was now going to determine the policies of a central government dominated by Buganda. The DP won both seats. The victories of the Democratic party in Toro and Bunyoro were perhaps the clearest illustrations of the widespread resentment of the KY-UPC alliance outside Buganda.

The situation was far from improved when Dr. Obote included five Kabaka Yekka members in his fifteen-member cabinet. In addition, Kabaka Yekka members were given the two key ministries of finance and economic development. Becoming minister of finance was the Hon. Mr. A. K. Sampa, a former minister of finance in Buganda government and one of the most outspoken Buganda secessionists in 1959-1961. He was also an avowed supporter of the Kabaka. The Hon. Mr. Simpson became minister of economic affairs and industries. The other three Kabaka Yekka members were given the very important ministries of education, health and works and communications. The Hon. Dr. J. S. L. Zake was named minister of education; the Hon. Dr. E. B. S. Lumu, a well-known medical doctor in Buganda, was appointed the minister of health; and the Hon. Mr. L. Kalule-Settala became minister of works and communications. It is important to note that these ministries involved activities that could be easily felt and understood by the common man. To the peasantry, neither the politics of foreign affairs, nor the politics of the ministry of information, broadcasting and tourism really counted, as long as radio Uganda continued to broadcast news and play good music. As a result, the KY's acquisition of the ministries of health, education, finance, works and communications and economic development amplified the Democratic party candidates' allegations that through the UPC alliance with Kabaka Yekka, Obote had "sold" Uganda to the Kabaka of Buganda. Feelings were aggravated when the five Kabaka Yekka members, upon selection to Obote's cabinet, immediately went to the Kabaka to swear their allegiance to the Kabaka's throne. Mr. A. L. Richards, referring to these five officials, in 1962, stated that "it seems clear that these ministers were regarded as being servants of the Kabaka, for all of them did the traditional obeisance and swearing of homage to him in the Great Lukiiko hall on being appointed as ministers to the Uganda government."[3]

The photographs of the five ministers, including Mr. Simpson, lying prostrate on the floor in front of the Kabaka not only appeared in the local press of Buganda but also were seen in national papers and magazines. Mr. J. T. Simpson was a European businessman in Uganda for over thirty years, and he had stood successfully as a Kabaka Yekka candidate. The five ministers had been appointed by Obote but their immediate return to the Kabaka was an act of political significance. It was questioned if they were going to be, in fact, Kabaka's servants or if they were going to be government ministers under Prime Minister Milton Obote. All in all, Obote was in for a delicate and very difficult time. It did not matter whether the alliance was or was not a marriage of convenience from Dr. Obote's point of view.

In spite of the UPC alliance with Kabaka Yekka, Dr. Obote, in my opinion, was no less a nationalist whose goal was to build a united Uganda. It seems to me that

Dr. Obote was taking a gamble when he allied the UPC with the KY. He seriously hoped and prayed that the gamble would be successful. There was strong evidence to believe that Dr. Obote viewed his alliance as the only conceivable way that the Buganda Kingdom could be readily associated with a central government. The association was urgently needed and necessary for Uganda to attain independence on schedule as one country with some form of nationalistic leadership.

The alliance and participation of traditional leaders gave Dr. Obote and his government a sense of legitimacy and acceptance in Buganda. Fearing to jeopardize his newly acquired acceptance in Buganda, Dr. Obote did not campaign in any way on behalf of the UPC to destroy the fears and rumors spread by the Democratic party that he had "sold" Uganda to the Kabaka. Dr. Obote was too shrewd and too farsighted to take chances on this issue. He wanted to buy time for what he had declared as his paramount aim--"the creation of a commonwealth of interests for the peoples of Uganda."

It is very difficult to say what exactly was on Dr. Obote's mind during the first four years after independence. Mr. Martin Lowenkopf, for instance, portrays Dr. Milton Obote as an astute professional politician who is one of the most skilled parliamentary debators in East Africa, but whose manner is reserved even with closest friends.[4] Dr. Obote may be the kind of man who keeps all his more profound thoughts to himself while speaking from the front of his head. Nevertheless, Dr. Obote stands out as a skilled politician that Uganda needed very much at the time of drastic political change.

Faced with the realities of no national consensus, no politically significant multiple group membership and multiple loyalties in the country, Obote as a nationalist found himself calmly swallowing all the criticisms that he had made an alliance on Kabaka Yekka's terms--terms which repudiated Obote's own principles and the principles upon which the Uganda Peoples Congress was founded.

Dr. Obote was not sacrificing but merely postponing his nationalistic goals in order to allow for the time needed for the development of a national consensus. He therefore saw and appreciated the need for a federation and the Uganda Constitution of 1962 which provided a political system loose enough not to antagonize the major ethnic groups (particularly Buganda Kingdom). However, through time, national loyalties would have emerged out of the central government's responsiveness to those interests and expectations widely held in all parts of Uganda.

The expansion of primary, secondary and university education was bound not only to spread but also to incorporate fundamental values of social justice, individual rights, membership group activities and free and popular political participation among the peoples of Uganda. The mobilization of science and modern technology against disease, poverty, infant mortality, ignorance, water shortages and cultural unawareness would also contribute to some extent toward acceptance of the national government as well as national politics.

In general, some European ideas, techniques and institutions would have helped the process of bringing all Ugandans to a realization of common purposes, wants, and goals which would eventually have led to a willingness of the people to be organized on the basis of national rather than ethnic group goals and past glories.

Apparently, Dr. Obote was attempting a policy of gradual national awareness that would eventually lead to one Uganda--a process he viewed as one that was to be guided, sometimes delayed or speeded up depending on circumstances. But the political history of Uganda was soon to leave no room for gradual advancement of nationalistic political changes.

The political events of 1962 to 1966 seem to prove Mr. Low to be correct. "In Uganda, they accommodate themselves to one major, ineluctable fact about Uganda's political history--that each phase of it has (so far) been profoundly conditioned by elements surviving from earlier phases."[5]

The issue of the "Lost Counties" has been one of the most crucial political disputes in Uganda since 1884-1886. In March, 1962, Mr. Kiwanuka, the president of the Democratic party, proposed that the pending elections should not be held in Bunyoro, Ankole, Toro and Busoga Kingdoms until the issue of the "Lost Counties" was resolved. The governor over-ruled him and the UPC managed to make political gains out of the affair by accusing Kiwanuka of trying to delay the elections and the independence of Uganda. Kiwanuka's Democratic party carried Bunyoro Kingdom in the 1962 national and local elections. The UPC candidates lost in Bunyoro, but the UPC paved the way for the alliance with Buganda Kingdom--an alliance that enabled Dr. Obote to form the national government.

All the rhetoric of independence and the independence-struggle-inspired enthusiasm for the themes of democracy, justice, freedom, liberty, and self-determination led the "Lost Counties" issue to become the most critical and potentially explosive dispute in Uganda immediately after independence. As soon as the African leaders who had spoken very highly of justice, freedom, liberty and <u>self-determination</u> took the reins of power, Bunyoro Kingdom pressed her demands for the immediate resolution of the "Lost Counties" issue. Dr. Milton Obote, as prime minister of Uganda, took the necessary steps to insure a fair and just settlement of the issue.

In the meantime, Sir Edward Mutesa II, the Kabaka of Buganda, was elected the president of Uganda in October, 1963. As president of Uganda and Kabaka of Buganda, Mutesa II, his chiefs and the Buganda Lukiiko made Buganda's mind known. As far as Buganda and the Kabaka were concerned, the "Lost Counties" issue would neither be discussed nor considered. The so-called "Lost Counties" were an integral part of Buganda Kingdom, the Baganda chiefs declared in their speeches around Buganda. The idea that, what was acquired through bloodshed can only be taken away through bloodshed was not only the gossip of 1960-1964 in Buganda but also an official closing statement of inflammatory speeches delivered by Saza and Gombolola chiefs in Buganda. I personally attended two public rallies in 1964 during which Saza chiefs concluded their speeches with the above quotation in such a way as to imply that the statement was a message from the Kabaka. Meanwhile, the Kabaka was spending the greater part of 1963 in the disputed teritories, Ndaiga in particular, where he was supervising political, social and land schemes for the resettlement of Buganda's veterans of World War II on the land. The veterans were mainly traditionalist Baganda who had fought along the British and allied forces in World War II. Clearly, the Kabaka was making it known directly that what was being said by his chiefs around Buganda was nothing short of his policy statement.

In the meantime, Kabaka Yekka was having internal problems. The main purposes for which Kabaka Yekka was founded were to unseat the Democratic party and to ensure that the Kabaka remained the only top source of power. Mr. Kiwanuka and his Democratic party had been defeated and the Kabaka was the president of Uganda. The two main bases of unity between Baganda traditional leaders and progressive, educated Baganda had been satisfied.

The traditionalists and neo-traditionalists, in particular the Saza and Gombolola chiefs, wanted to dominate the leadership of Kabaka Yekka as a means of preserving the traditional hierarchical power structure. The progressives, like Abu Mayanja, a lawyer, E. M. K. Mulira, J. W. Kiwanuka, Dr. Luyimbazi Zake, I. K. Musazi and others who had tried to establish political parties in the 1950's, were trying to prepare for reforms of the existing political system of Buganda, hoping to make it in time a representative government.

The traditionalists had earlier needed the relatively more educated Baganda's help in Buganda's battle for a full federal status. The progressives, too, had depended on the Kabaka's personal approval and the support of the traditionalists in their bid for Buganda's seats in the National Assembly. The progressives, therefore, had been selected by the Buganda Lukiiko to represent Buganda in the National Assembly, while the traditionalists had been successful in fulfilling their goal of full federal status for the Buganda Kingdom.

The new feeling of relatively less need for each other's support, resulting from each acquiring almost all the intended goals, made the future of Kabaka Yekka uncertain. But one thing was absolutely clear as it had always been--the Kabaka's avowed men, the traditionalists, had over 95 per cent of the support of the masses in Buganda. Kabaka Yekka had neither a president nor a chairman until September, 1962. Before this, Kabaka Yekka was based purely on consensus and the Kabaka as the implied head of the party. The first climax of progressives vs. traditionalists came in September, 1962, when the Kabaka himself intervened in the selection of the first KY chairman. He supported Michael Kintu, then Buganda prime minister and acknowledged leader of the traditionalists and neo-traditionalists in Buganda. Kintu became the first chairman of Kabaka Yekka.

Matters became worse when progressive elements in Kabaka Yekka suggested that Buganda government should be developed into a representative government, removed from Saza chiefs and with the cabinet being elected by the Lukiiko and fully responsible to the Lukiiko. They also dared to point out that land reforms in Buganda were overdue and that Kabaka Yekka should be transformed into a real political party. The progressives, through their calls for reforms, had made themselves the enemies of the established hierarchical power structure of Buganda. Drastic changes within Kabaka Yekka were bound to take place at this point, and one course of action was clear. The progressives had to move out of the Kabaka Yekka or the traditionalists would kick them out.

The progressive defections began in 1962. Joseph W. Kiwanuka resigned from Kabaka Yekka and joined Uganda Peoples Congress in protest of the traditionalist domination of Kabaka Yekka. In February, 1962, K. Musazi, who was advocating land reforms in Buganda, resigned from Kabaka Yekka in protest to what he called "the machinery of the Kabaka's government which was subservient to an establishment clique whose objects are divorced from the interests of the people of the country."[6]

The forces opposing political changes within Buganda Kingdom were as powerful as ever, and they were driving the progressives out of the party. Furthermore, the progressives generally were the educated from whom the Lukiiko had chosen Buganda's representatives to the National Assembly. The traditionalists in Buganda government would have liked to have been elected to Parliament, but they had great difficult with the English language--the only language used in Parliament. The breakdown of communication between the most important progressives in the National Assembly and Kabaka Yekka, which was the party of the Kabaka and his chiefs as well as the masses who had very little knowledge of the implications of political change, was driving Buganda toward isolationist defensive attitudes. The most important thing to conclude from these conflicts was that the 21 votes of Buganda in the National Assembly were no longer a solid base on which the Kabaka, his chiefs and masses in Buganda could count. At the same time, since the beginning of 1963, the UPC had been working hard in Buganda, directly trying to establish itself as a political party in Buganda in spite of Kabaka Yekka's severe charges that UPC political activities in Buganda constituted a breach of the 1961 alliance. The UPC had agreed not to sponsor any independent candidates in Buganda and also UPC activities in Buganda were supposed to be in direct support of Kabaka Yekka.

It was under these circumstances that the "Lost Counties" issue irreversibly gravitated toward a climax. This conflict which had persisted throughout the colonial period was now extremely critical and could neither be postponed nor resolved without spelling doom for the delicate Kabaka Yekka alliance with Obote's Uganda Peoples Congress.

The "Lost Counties" issue had to be resolved as soon as possible or else, as stated by the British Privy Councillors report of May, 1962, the issue would lead to civil war in Uganda.

> It is not necessary to imagine the two kingdoms raising armies in order to invade each other. Events would probably follow a different and

sadly familiar course. First there would be increased agitation by Bunyoro in Mubende District; that would be met by repression on the part of police and magistrates; violence would follow, the agitators would seek and obtain support and recruits from their sympathizers in Bunyoro. The two governments would support their own tribesmen, at first covertly and then overtly. Civil strife would gradually develop into a civil war, which would not be confined to the disputants if the Bunyoro succeeded in enlisting the support of neighboring tribes.[7]

In the 1920's the Bunyoro population in Mubende District established a Mubende-Bunyoro committee whose purpose was to fight for a return of the counties to Bunyoro. These committees had maintained pressure in spite of British declarations since 1900 that the status of the counties was permanently settled by the 1900 Uganda Agreement which defined the Buganda Kingdom boundaries. In 1963 the Kabaka was carrying out massive resettlement of the disputed counties with Baganda veterans--people who were proud that they had proven themselves excellent fighters in World War II. The veterans also did not hesitate to tell the Bunyoro that they could start fighting any time they felt like it. Given the conditions and prediction of the British Privy Councillors report, Dr. Obote saw no solution better than a free and fair referendum. It was therefore primarily over the "Lost Counties" issue that the alliance of UPC and KY disintegrated.

On August 24, 1964, Prime Minister Obote announced to the National Assembly the dissolution of the alliance between Kabaka Yekka and the UPC. He immediately dropped from the cabinet two Kabaka Yekka ministers, Amos Sampa, ex-minister of finance in Buganda and a secessionist who had been minister of finance in Obote's government; and J. S. Mayanja-Nkangi, minister of commerce and industry, who became prime minister in the Kabaka's government. The Kabaka Yekka members of Parliament crossed the floor to the opposition but no alliance could be worked out with the Democratic party. A day later, August 25, all Kabaka Yekka members walked out of Parliament to protest as the National Assembly approved a government motion setting November 4, 1964, as the date for a referendum in the "Lost Counties" of Buyaga and Bugangazzi where serious trouble was imminent.

The decision of Dr. Obote's government to proceed with the referendum arrangements for Buyaga and Bugangazzi counties brought the UPC-KY alliance to an end and opened the door to direct and open confrontation between the Kabaka and Dr. Obote.

August 31, 1964, was a momentous day in the political history of Uganda. Abu Mayanja, the legal adviser to Kabaka Yekka and minister of education in Buganda, was elected by the Buganda Lukiiko to represent Northeast Kyaggwe in the National Assembly. Mayanja, a Kabaka Yekka spokesman and yet a nationalist, was replacing J. T. Simpson who had resigned his seat when Kabaka Yekka decided to go into the opposition. More important than Abu Mayanja's appointment on that day was that all Kabaka Yekka members

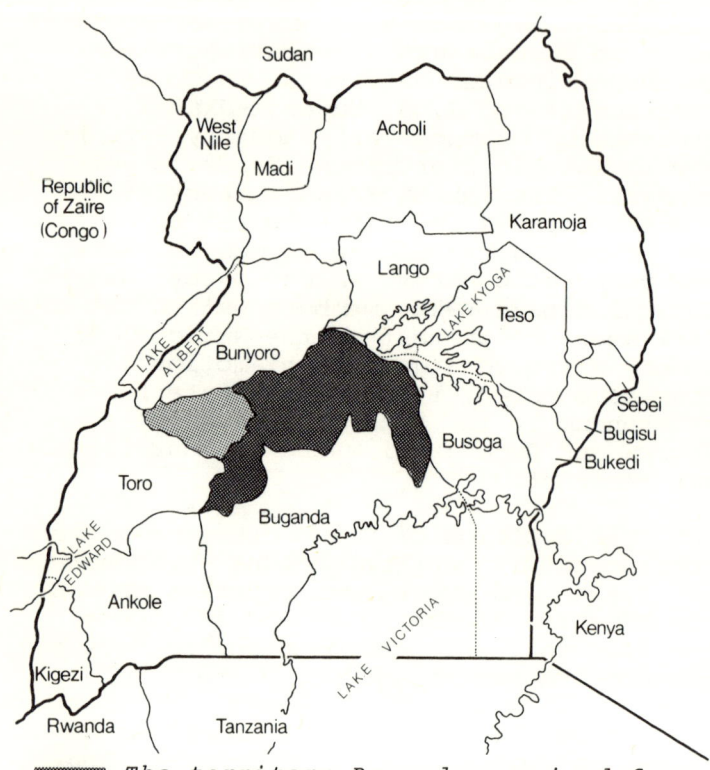

■ The territory Buganda acquired from her neighbors during the British colonization of Uganda (1884-1890)

▨ Buyaga and Bugangazzi Counties which the Privy Councillors' Report of May 1962 recommended to be returned to Bunyoro Kingdom. Approx. 80% of the people in these counties are Banyoro It was for these areas that a referendum was held in Nov. 4, 1964.

of Parliament furiously walked out of the
National Assembly, as the assembly passed
the enabling bill for the November 4 referendum in the "Lost Counties."

Adding fuel to the fire was the provision of the bill that only those registered
in the disputed counties in the April,1962
elections could vote in the referendum;
this meant (and purposely meant) that the
Kabaka's 4,500 veterans and other Baganda,
to whom the Kabaka had given land and settled in the area since independence under
the Ndaiga settlement scheme, were to be
excluded from voting. In the United States
a president declares that he will not be
the first president to bring American soldiers home in defeat; in Buganda Kingdom
the Kabaka could not stand the slightest
thought that he would be the king who had
to part with an inch of Buganda Kingdom.

The referendum provided three choices for the people who were living in the
"Lost Counties" before 1962. (1) They
could choose to remain an integral part of
Buganda Kingdom; (2) choose to become part
of Bunyoro Kingdom; (3) choose to form an
independent district of their own. With a
very large percentage of Banyoro in both
counties Buyaga and Bugangazzi, it was apparent that the counties were bound to return to Bunyoro Kingdom. The Kabaka and
his people had never had a better cause
for an almost unanimous commitment to
secede from Uganda. It should be noted
that from the results of the first national
elections of 1961, in which only 3 per cent
of Buganda voted, one can say with absolute
certainty that over 90 per cent of more
than two million people in Buganda were
solidly behind the Kabaka. In Buganda over

ninety-five per cent of the population are small farmers.[8] Practically all farmers were solidly behind the Kabaka and the traditionalists of Buganda's informal and formal leadership.

The referendum bill was presented to the president who, as was expected by most Ugandans, refused to sign the bill into law. Sir Edward Mutesa II was both the Kabaka of Buganda and president of Uganda. Upon the president's refusal to sign, the prime minister signed in accordance with the constitution. Uganda's political crisis was at a bursting point, and an all-out clash between Obote and the Kabaka was imminent.

The referendum took place according to plan and the two counties voted for returning to the jurisdiction of the king of Bunyoro. Dr. Obote formalized the results of the referendum into law. Seven Bunyoro officials, trying to administer the area where the Kabaka of Buganda had built his Ndaiga residence, were shot and killed by Buganda veterans in December, 1964, a month after the referendum.[9] Bunyoro Kingdom legislature responded by voting to demand the removal of certain personal property of the Kabaka. Meanwhile, Baganda chiefs in the dispute areas were arresting, trying and sentencing those Banyoro who resisted the day-to-day administration on behalf of the Kabaka.

It was precisely during this period of serious political tension and the power struggle between Prime Minister Obote and the Kabaka of Buganda, who was also president of Uganda, that charges were brought in Parliament against Prime Minister Obote, Army Chief of Staff Colonel Idi

Amin, Onama, minister of defense and Odoko Neykon, minister and a personal friend of Obote, that they had made illict deals in ivory, gold and coffee amounting to $357,000, with the Congolese rebels.[10] The charges were the turning point in Uganda's politics. Corruption charges were politically important but not as critical as the fact that the Kabaka and his supporters were resolved to use the opportunity fairly or unfairly to oust Prime Minister Obote.

On the national front Kabaka Yekka Secretary General Daudi Ocheng, member of Parliament, moved a motion in Parliament on February 4, 1965, calling for an immediate inquiry into the alleged gold, ivory and coffee smuggling affair. In a state of uncertainty, confusion and fear, the motion was supported on both sides of the house and passed with only one dissenting vote. Members of Parliament, even close personal friends and political allies of Dr. Obote, supported the motion, afraid of being caught in the middle of the situation. They did not know whether the allegations were true or false. At this time Dr. Obote was out of the capital on a "meet the people tour" in Northern Uganda. On February 10, the Democratic party president demanded to know when the commission of inquiry, in accord with the assembly's February 4 resolution, would be appointed. Two weeks from the day of the resolution, while Dr. Obote was still upcountry, Daudi Ocheng, secretary general of Kabaka Yekka, demanded the immediate resignation of Dr. Obote because, as prime minister, he had failed to carry out the resolution of Parliament calling for the inquiry. Ocheng's motion in the National Assembly did not only demand the resignation of Obote but also the resignation of Onama, minister of defense and Adoko Neykon, minister of planning and community development.

It was in this atmosphere of political trouble and uncertainty that Dr. Obote made the claim that the Kabaka had requested military assistance from foreign diplomats, with the intent of overthrowing the Uganda government.

The facts of what really went on between February, 1965, and March, 1966, are very hard to establish. Probably, Obote's allegation that Kabaka was planning to overthrow the Uganda government can be accepted as reasonably true, for the Kabaka did admit later that he had contacted some foreign embassies for assistance, if the need did arise. The facts known are:

(1) That there was no hope of reconciling the Kabaka with Prime Minister Obote.

(2) That Dr. Obote's own position in Parliament was very insecure.

(3) That the legality of Obote's suspension of the 1962 constitution was challenged in the Uganda High Court by Kabaka Yekka, but the chief justice had already sworn allegiance to Obote's new constitution and new government. The challenge was a failure.

(4) That between February, 1965 and March, 1966, the Kabaka of Buganda petitioned the United Nations, the British government and the Organization of African Unity to intervene and restore Uganda to the democracy of the 1962 constitution. None of the organizations responded.

It does, therefore, appear that the circumstances at the time, from Obote's point of view, necessitated a revolution to prevent a coup by the Kabaka or a rebellion and secession of Buganda.

On February 22, 1966, Prime Minister Obote ordered the arrest of Ibingira and four other ministers. At the time of his arrest, Ibingira was not only minister of state, but also secretary general of the ruling Uganda Peoples Congress. Ibingira and the other arrested ministers were UPC members who had supported the resolution in Parliament calling for an inquiry and the resignation of Obote. With the arrest of the five ministers, Obote began a revolution in the name of national unity and stability.

On February 24, Obote declared that he was assuming all governmental powers. On February 26, Dr. Obote declared that the 1962 constitution and Parliament were suspended. While on March 7, 1966, Obote brought in judges and lawyers from Kenya and Tanzania to conduct an impartial inquiry in the alleged illicit dealing in Congolese gold and ivory, he went ahead to consolidate his own political position. By April, 1966, Obote had imposed his own constitution, making himself president of Uganda and head of the military. At this point it was beyond doubt that Buganda Kingdom would make secession moves. Dr. Obote had already demonstrated his power over Buganda Kingdom and the Kabaka. The suspension of Parliament and the 1962 constitution also meant that Buganda's clear legal guarantees of full federal status were no longer in force. Buganda had survived British power. It was, therefore, inconceivable to most Baganda, particularly the traditional authority of Buganda, that Dr. Obote's power could challenge the Kabaka's power.

On May 20, 1966, Christopher Kaggiwa, a close friend of the Kabaka, moved a motion in Buganda Lukiiko ordering the central government off Buganda soil. The motion carried, ordering all central government personnel and property out of Buganda Kingdom by May 30, 1966. In other words, Buganda was declaring itself to be an independent state within ten days and ordering the national government out of Kampala, the commercial, industrial, educational, political, and communication center of Uganda. It should be emphasized here that Buganda Kingdom is in the central part of the country and Buganda covers one-fourth of the whole country. More than that, Buganda, according to the *London Times*, is the economic hub and the commercial centre. Secession would have a more damaging effect on Uganda than Katanga's secession had on the Congo.[11]

The Buganda government's resolution of May 20, 1966, marked the beginning of a state of rebellion, for when a few Baganda chiefs were arrested by the central government for their inflammatory speeches in context of the Lukiiko resolution, revolts started all across Buganda. Violence broke out in Kampala on May 23, and rumors spread all over the country that fire arms flowed from the Kabaka's palace to Baganda veterans and peasants who were to be the backbone of Buganda's military strength. The circumstances forced Dr. Obote to order a siege of Mango Hill, the location of the Kabaka's palace, to confiscate the arms of the secessionist. In a sense, Dr. Obote's order to lay siege to the Kabaka's palace on May 24, 1966, was an absolutely necessary action because if the peasants and veterans had been given arms they would undoubtedly have fought to the last man defending their Kabaka. Obote's action was prudent in terms of keeping to a minimum the loss of Ugandan lives and preservation of national unity and stability.

The Buganda prime minister's statement of 1962 on behalf of all Baganda except a few hundred of well educated Baganda should be remembered. "From time immemorial the Baganda have known no other ruler above their Kabaka in his kingdom, and still they do not recognize any other person whose authority does not derive from the Kabaka and is exercised on his behalf."[12]

Only one conclusion can be drawn. It was unquestionable that the attack against the Kabaka meant a dangerous step against the deep-rooted loyalty of the overwhelming majority of Buganda. Obote, in the name of national unity and stability, ordered the siege of Kabaka's palace, but in doing so, Obote made himself the arch enemy of at least 95 per cent of the people in Buganda, about one-fourth of the Ugandan electorate.

A state of emergency was declared in Buganda on May 24, 1966. Two days after the emergency was declared, the Kabaka and his government were defeated at a cost of 200 to 1000 Ugandan lives.[13] With the downfall of the traditional leadership in Buganda at Mengo Hill and its aftermath, it became an absolute certainty that Buganda would be impossible for Obote to rule without intensive use of military and police force.

Dr. Obote, like everybody else at the time, knew that his takeover of all political powers in Uganda, his suspension of the elected Parliament and the 1962 Uganda Constitution were all unconstitutional actions. In order to legitimatize his actions, Obote stressed in a series of nationally televised speeches that he had been forced to act in the name of national unity and stability to prevent a coup by the Kabaka. The rationalization of his actions to the people of Uganda could have created support for him outside of Buganda for, after all, the Kabaka and Baganda were not politically popular outside Buganda. But the people's loyalties, especially in the kingdoms of Bunyoro, Ankole, Toro and Busogo, were not with national causes but with their respective kings.

To the masses in the other kingdoms, the downfall of the Kabaka did not come to mean a downfall of an enemy but a downfall of a great symbol of traditional rule. Since Obote could dethrone a king so powerful as was the Kabaka of Buganda, then the masses reasonsed, their own leaders were in real danger from Obote. In addition, the suspension of the constitution was in itself a threat to the semifederal status of the kingdoms of Ankole, Toro, Bunyoro and Busoga. In short, Obote could neither create support out of the hatred of Buganda and Kabaka nor depend on the Uganda Peoples Congress. He could not depend on the party because on February 22, he had ordered the arrest of Ibingira, Secretary General of UPC and four other ministers who had a popular following within the UPC. There was therefore too much fragmentation and confusion within the party for anybody to depend on it as a basis for political power. In other words, the siege of Mengo Hill had put Uganda on the road that was, out of necessity, bound to lead to a political system in Uganda that is, both in theory and practice, a unitary form of government based on the use of military and police force.

Dr. Obote had unsuccessfully tried to displace and transform the traditionalists vs. nationalists struggle for power into Buganda secession vs. the rest of Uganda and national unity. It seems certain that the political history of Uganda, the immovable ethnic group loyalties and the absence of anything that could be considered as a national consensus in Uganda before and after independence made it necessary for a nationalist like Dr. Obote to impose a unitary form of government on the people of Uganda in the interest of all Ugandans, including Baganda. The irony of Uganda's post-independence politics is that a government whose basis is force had to be imposed on the people in the name of the people. In other words, Obote used force against the people for the people and in the economic interest of all the peoples of Uganda.

In order to understand that from Obote's point of view force was appropriately used against the people in the name of the people, one has to know what the interests of the people have been and continue to be; and to know what the interests of the people have been is to know what all Ugandans used to talk about whenever they discussed independence. Independence seemed to have meant different things to different people.

Independence for some members of the educated elite meant acquisition of prestigious positions originally held by the British. For the peasantry, independence was first and foremost the return to traditional authority and secondly the economic or material betterment of their lives. The main desires independence meant to the overwhelming majority of Ugandans were:

1. Higher prices for crops, particularly coffee, cotton and teac.

2. Ownership of and opportunity to run mills to grind corn or cassava into flour, coffee processing factories and cotton gins.

3. Raise in salaries and wages and creation of more jobs.

4. Free medical care and health services to reach all citizens.

5. More schools, especially in rural areas; free primary, secondary and university education was expected.

6. Acquisition of more African teachers, nurses, and other professionals and artisans plus very rapid Africanization or Ugandanization.

7. Opportunities for better houses, better roads leading to and from all villages, and better water supplies (water pumps were in great demand in most parts of Uganda).

In other words, the people of Uganda can best be described as both "transitionals" and "moderns" in their thinking. That is, they are by custom loyal to their traditional societies and traditional forms of government, but their minds are in search of a material world better than the traditional set-up can provide. In a sense all the people in Uganda are in motion--moving towards a new world--a world of material comfort. The peasantry--as well as the educated elite--want a new material world, and they want it as soon as possible. But the masses as a whole lack the awareness of the relationship between their desires or hopes and the means to the goals.

The needs of the masses amount to one common desire--a strong desire for rapid modernization. But the masses are completely unaware of the fact that the common desire for rapid modernization make modernizing leadership, national unity and stability necessary. The peasantry and traditionalists are in a kind of a dilemma. Their minds, tastes, desires, goals and dreams are for modernization, while their political loyalties are still committed to the traditional values and institutions of government. The process of rapid industrialization involves very rapid and drastic changes, and drastic changes are always painful. The leaders find themselves forced to take unpopular positions to keep the process going. For instance, had Buganda succeeded, secession would have amounted to nothing short of economic suicide, for Buganda is too small to have an internal market sufficient to allow for rapid economic growth. In addition, light industries in Buganda depend entirely on electricity generated just outsi-e of Buganda at Jinja. Most important is the fact that Uganda is surrounded by Kenya, Tanzania, Congo-Kinshasha and Sudan, states under the control of staunch nationalists. Being completely landlocked, Buganda cannot survive economically for her entire economy depends on exports of coffee and cotton. Therefore, it becomes appropriate to assert that under the circumstances the imposition of a unitary government in Uganda is completely against the popular view of the people, but it still serves the interests of all Uganda, particularly Buganda, whose economy is dynamic within Uganda.

The changes that have taken place in Uganda since independence have been drastic changes involving value systems and the traditional social structures. Since the traditional leaders and institutions could not give the right of way to modernizing leadership without a fight, the necessary changes have taken place violently and at a high price in terms of human suffering and accumulation of grievances against the central government. Since the peasantry make up about 95 per cent of the population, the nationalists in power found themselves compelled to use force on the masses for compliance. Uganda has consolidated a modernizing leadership and is in the process of creating a national bureaucracy which will mobilize both the material and human resources to effect rapid industrialization --the rapid industrialization that is urgently needed by all Ugandans.

    The process of modernization involves serious contradictions. The overwhelming majority of people want their traditional forms of government, but their material needs amount to nothing less than a genuine desire for rapid industrialization, which in turn necessitates not only modernizing leadership and a united Uganda at the expense of the traditional centers of power, but also a national bureaucracy that can manipulate the material and the human resources of Uganda.

    With this understanding, one can say that Obote's government was responsible for and responsive to the needs of the people. And yet, there was growing fear and frustration throughout the country, for neither were the material needs met, nor could the peasantry abandon their loyalty to their deposed traditional leaders. Hence, the national government found itself compelled to continue using force against the people, in the name of the people and national unity. Worst of all, the force used to keep the country together did not seem to establish a consensus but hastened the breakdown of whatever semblances would have taken root. The extensive lack of confidence in the national government by the people, particularly the peasantry, was evident in the periodic outbreaks of violence and attempts on the Ugandan president's life in December, 1969.

Between 1966 and 1970 coups against the national government were attempted by the remnants of organized traditional leaders and the peasantry. On June 22, 1967, twenty-two persons were arrested for planning a coup between February 14 and 18. Christmas, 1969, Dr. Obote was shot as he was leaving the national convention of his own party--the Uganda Peoples Congress. Dr. Obote's government was effective in crushing attempted coups and proved active and efficient in rounding up so-called political undesirables. But in the process, the national government increased tension and hostility between itself and the majority of the people.

From the point of view of the material needs of all Uganda, Dr. Obote's government was doing a very good job. According to the national statistics, medical services have more than tripled since independence in 1962. Primary and secondary education has been extended to most parts of the country and Makerere University facilities have been expanded and improved to accommodate twice as many students as they did at the time of independence. The gross national product was increasing at a rate of 10 to 12 per cent per year compared to less than 4 per cent before independence. The second five-year plan seemed to be more ambitious for it projected higher growth rates in all sectors of the national economy by 1975.[14] At independence, Uganda produced about 50 per cent of the milk locally consumed, and according to the plan, she is now producing 100 per cent of the milk consumed in Uganda; by

1972 Uganda will be in a position to export milk and milk products. Obviously, Dr. Obote seriously meant what he said in his official New Year's message delivered to the nation on December 31, 1969.

> In Uganda, the last ten years have been years of unqualified success and unprecedented development. In this short space of time, we have shaken off the colonial yoke, shattered the shackles of feudalism and we are rapidly breaking the back of ignorance, poverty, and disease. In spite of several setbacks we are rapidly achieving our national goal, which is to build a united, peaceful, happy and prosperous nation.[15]

Dr. Obote seemed to have good reasons to be optimistic, but as far as the peasantry was and is concerned, there was hardly any economic growth; for progress to them can only be seen in terms of their main cash crops--cotton and coffee. Unfortunately, the coffee and cotton prices have been on the decline since independence. In any case, the masses did not seem to be willing to forget their ungracefully ousted traditional leaders in exchange for material benefits. They wanted both and they did not see the inherent contradictions involved.

After a careful examination of the problem of leadership and of building a national government in Uganda, I am inclined to make a few generalizations. The primary needs of the total population of Uganda are material. The material needs in themselves amount to a decision for rapid modernization on behalf of the total population. The urgent attempts to industrialize necessitate a consolidation of leadership that is dedicated to national unity and specific national programs of industrialization. The success of the plan depends upon national unity and the extent to which the national leadership can manipulate both material and human resources in the entire society.

Since the early stages of moderniation were full of contradictions and painful experiences for the people, it was almost inevitable that the national government would find itself repeatedly compelled to resort to force to bring about compliance. In short, Uganda, in the process of modernization, needed leadership of planners who were not only responsive to the material needs of the people, but were also determined to carry through the plans of development in time of negative responses from the masses and traditional power structures. All in all, it appeared that Obote had little choice but to accept a new role, a role of a dictator based on the themes of one party, one government, one Parliament and one people. Since the siege of the Kabaka's palace, Uganda under Milton Obote was for some years destined to be an authoritarian, highly centralized political system, a political system ready to use force and to depend on force to keep Uganda in one piece in order to allow time for the cultivation of a national consensus.

The prospects of Obote and his government generating a national consensus through time and an all-out effort to industrialize the country are the subject of the next chapter.

6

Obote's Government and the Creation of National Consensus

Full and sensitive awareness and appreciation of the bulwark of ethnic group nationalism (centered around the deposed kings of Buganda, Bunyoro, Ankole, Toro and Busoga and on the political parochialism based on the historical and the social and political colonial experiences of the other parts of Uganda) make this study incomplete without a sympathetic but critical examination of what prospects existed for Obote and his government--prospects to generate support for himself and for the central government. Consequently, I find it not

only necessary but inevitable that I have
to involve myself with some kind of specu-
lations and predictions. I am aware of
the fact that there are latent forces at
work within the political system of Uganda. It may also be unrealistic for one to
venture into the realm of predictions
when dealing with a young nation like
Uganda.

Nevertheless it is my contention
that through a careful and critical examination of the relationships between demands,[1] outputs[2] and feedback,[3] as suggested by David Easton[4] (systems analysis),
one can have a sound and relatively reliable basis for predictions. What the
<u>systems analysis</u> means, for instance, is
that when the people of former Bunyoro
Kingdom desire numerous water holes in
their country and ask the Uganda government to provide the means to dig them,
their request constitutes an <u>input</u> into the
political system. The government decision
to construct the water holes and means used
to carry out the decision constitutes an
<u>output</u> of the political system. If the co
construction of water holes pleases the
people of Bunyoro and they decide to support the government, their satisfaction and
support constitutes <u>feedback</u> to the political system. In other words, by viewing
what all Ugandans expect from the government and what the government is able and
willing to give to the people, one can assess the conditions Obote's government had
to create--a material and political culture, with concomitant institutions, values and conflicts, through which a planned,
guided, speeded up or delayed national culture could be mothered and nursed to maturity.

As already expressed in different ways, the people of Uganda are caught between two worlds, the world of new material needs and the world of traditions and customs. Most unfortunately for Uganda's hope for consensus the overwhelming majority of the people of Uganda are unaware of their dual existence. Very few Karamojong would not welcome the idea of government digging water holes for their cattle, but very few Karamojong would welcome continued government presence in Karamojong country. The peoples of former Buganda Kingdom want education, better roads and more business in and outside the capital of Uganda, but they are not ready to accept the consequences of these activities that inevitably lead to intermingling of the peoples of Uganda, making it necessary to have a central government serving over every Ugandan.

The purpose of this chapter is to evaluate the possibilities that existed for Dr. Obote and his government to create higher loyalties which would supercede ethnic and other parochial loyalties in Uganda. The dual existence of the peoples of Uganda provided room for Dr. Obote and his government to reach the hearts of the peasantry in spite of their necessary break with their political past and Obote's unpopular complete political reconstruction of the country. The peoples of Uganda can be roused to a new social and political consciousness with dynamic awareness of the possibilities of change and progress.

Education

Free primary, secondary, university and technical education, as well as a rapid increase of schools, especially in rural areas was and still is a sure way to get to the hearts of the masses. The masses did not have formal education but they value beyond measure education for their children or grandchildren. Dr. Obote put it simply, clearly and correctly when he stated on August 18, 1969, "The popularity of education has grown in this country to such an extent that most people appear to be more interested in its availability than in its content."[5]

Most people in Uganda make little sense out of the content of education but they know that being educated means money, prestige, and often political power. Consequently, those who are too old or too deprived to be educated themselves, want it for their children, grandchildren and relatives. What formal education means to most Ugandans is well projected by Dr. Obote's remarks:

> In more than ten years that I have been a member of Uganda's legislature, I have observed that debates on educational policies have concentrated on the number of schools and school population, the spread of schools, the establishment of teacher training institutes, and rapid production of Ugandans trained as professionals and artisans. Outside the legislature there is a loud cry by parents for more primary and secondary schools in their localities. Every

end of January or beginning of
February the hearts of many parents
sink because their sons or daughters
have not been selected for admission
to secondary schools.[6]

The popularity of education is also
reflected by the fact that since independence the national government has been
devoting as much as 28 per cent of the
national budget to formal education and
training. It should be noted, in addition,
that there are no laws in Uganda obliging
young people to go to school, but still
all schools are crowded. Parents and
practically all young people in the country see it prudent for one to endure a
daily twelve-mile walk to and from school
in order to receive formal education or
training.

Education means so much to the peoples
of Uganda that it was no surprise when
Obote came out very strongly stating that,
"Education must be our first instrument--
the first national instrument--to arouse
and promote national consciousness. In
that way education will be Uganda's chosen
instrument for national-building, and
vigor of the young and the grown-ups to
accept, promote and manage it as the most
effective foundation for building the nation around national institutions."[7]

Unquestionably, formal education can
be an effective instrument for arousing a
new social and political consciousness of
the people. But given the other conditions
within Uganda, new social and political consciousness was not necessarily bringing
about a national consensus which was to
serve as a basis for a democratic

representative government under the leadership of Dr. Obote. All Ugandans seem to agree that formal education is good and desirable, but this does not mean that primary and secondary school graduates are destined to be men and women whose priorities are to advance national interests. Dr. Obote himself remarked, " . . . in my assessment we have not moved very far from the results of the education investments which the British wanted to get when they introduced formal education in Uganda."[8]

In other words, the content and goals of education, seven years after independence, have not significantly changed. To understand the nature and goals of colonial education is to become aware of the fact that national investments in education may not necessarily lead to the political and national consciousness or to the unity and political stability that is desired.

The colonial education was not meant to produce Ugandan citizens. As already established, the British found it cheaper to employ native hands as co-administrators. The British could not financially afford to bring all the artisans required to administer Uganda from Britain or India. So they opened up schools where the natives were taught to write, read, and speak English. The goal of colonial education was to produce indigenous helping hands to consolidate British rule. Natives were given a formal education so that they could be employed as interpretors, semi-skilled artisans to assist expatriates, tax collectors and assistants in the spread of Christianity. In other words, formal education was to produce people who were to be employed by government, local authorities, the commercial sector and the missionaries.

The nature of colonial education which continued after independence was likely to generate little support for Obote as well as for the central government.

How people view education may be one of the decisive factors in determining whether the spread of primary and secondary school education will become the backbone of nation building in Uganda.

> The image of education as a preparation for employment is so inclusive, extensive and deep-rooted, that everywhere in Uganda, if a secondary schoolboy in particular, or even a University graduate attempts to settle in the rural area and to do what the mass of the people are engaged in doing--farming--whispers ascending to unspeakable innuendoes and songs disparaging to the character of such a person, are all a certainty. The parents, the clan, neighbors, and various others will begin to say 'So and so's son has not got a job because of his character or because he has no brains.' So the educated lad flees from the rural area and rushes to town and in the town there is either no job or if there is one, it has a very limited security.[9]

It should be noted that by May, 1961, the per cent of African children of school age attending school in Uganda was 26.1 per cent in primary schools and 1.7 per cent in secondary schools.[10] Primary in this sense includes elementary schools providing the basic training and education to children within customary or compulsory ages of full-time education. Secondary schools include middle (junior secondary schools), secondary schhols and high schools. In other words, before independence less than 30 per cent of the African children of school age were attending school. Probably, the colonial government's policy was to educate only enough hands as it needed. But since independence the government has responded to the great demands for primary and secondary education.

In September, 1964, the Uganda government disclosed that 23 new senior secondary schools were to be added to the 43 existing schools by January, 1965, and that an additional 69 expatriate teachers were to be recruited. Most significant was the report of the minister of education, Dr. S. J. Luyimbazi-Zake, stating that he intended to have 6,000 pupils ready to start senior secondary schools in 1965 as against 3,000 in 1964.[11] The same year, the Uganda government announced that 2,000 Ugandans were to study abroad in the academic year, 1964-65.[12] Given the resources available, the government was doing its best in the area of education.

But by September, 1965, the Democratic party was accusing the government of having failed to meet the educational needs of the people. The Democratic party, being in the opposition, proposed in Parliament that the government provide free education throughout Uganda by January, 1966. The motion was defeated in the National Assembly after government spokesmen made it clear that state revenues could not possibly support such a scheme. By 1969, government sources were claiming that over 90 per cent of Uganda's school age children were attending school.

All in all, the government's performance in areas of education was outstanding. But the tremendous increases in educational opportunities have not been matched with increases in job opportunities. What this means is that (with the exception of professionals like medical doctors and lawyers who are in great demand and can employ themselves by establishing their own businesses) the most insecure person in Uganda is the educated and semi-educated man who finds himself uprooted by his education from the traditional style of living.

As early as 1967 the government and private investment sectors in the country were unable to absorb a sizeable portion of the high school graduates. Those who were unable to continue in higher institutions of learning and training and who were not employed immediately found themselves compelled to move into cities, particularly Kampala. A large number of primary and secondary graduates who found themselves uncomforatble in the rural culture and without security of employment and steady income in the urban areas become a significant source of political instability rather than a political force for national unity.

Unemployment is not the only problem resulting from rapid increase in educational opportunities. Education is a means to higher pay and status. As Ugandans acquired more education, skill and professional training, they become salaried employees and their steady income contributes significantly to the already sharp economic and cultural gap between the educated and the masses. According to Dr. Obote, "A cultural gap and wide disparity of incomes are now what Uganda needs. They are the bedrock of instability."[13]

Apparently Dr. Obote was aware and sensitive to the cultural and economic gap, but he did very little about it. Since independence, salaries have been increased rather than maintained or reduced. For instance, Dr. Obote found himself obligated to give material rewards through better pay to the army and police. Dr. Obote's power depended on the army and police whose lack of education and ideological and political commitments is self-evident. He had to increase their salaries as a means of keeping them satisfied and loyal to his government-- hence a defense budget of $17,025,000 in 1966, which is 10.2 per cent of the national budget and nearly as large as the combined defense budgets of Kenya and Tanzania.[14] In addition to the defense budgets were Dr. Obote's exorbitant expenditures on his 1,000-man presidential protection unit. The presidential protection unit, or "secret police," was formed immediately after an attempt on Dr. Obote's life in December, 1969. The head of the secret police was Dr. Obote's cousin and he earned more than $1400 per month. The national annual per capita income is $100.

To meet government expenditures Dr. Obote imposed higher taxes. The endless taxation resulted in higher prices of sugar, salt, rice, meat, medicine, clothing, etc. Meanwhile, the coffee and cotton prices have been falling and the farmers have been getting poorer. Widespread educational opportunities, better salaries for those who find employment, exorbitant expenditures for maintainance of the secret police and the rising cost of living but declining coffee and cotton prices (the main source of income for the masses) have only resulted in the widening of the cultural and economic gap--an event that was bound to maim the development of a national consensus.

Education has not only led to congested urban areas, with thousands of unemployed hands, but has also increased both social and physical mobility, resulting in intense competition for jobs, promotions, appointments and scholarships. In many cases, competition in these areas has taken on ethnic group overtures as a result of real and seomtimes imagined government policies. There are many Ugandans who have excused their failures in terms of ethnic group membership, saying that good posts, scholarships and promotions were for the Nilotics and not for the Baganda or Basoga.

Dr. Obote's government was responsive to the great demands for education. But it is difficult to say that through education alone a national consensus was forthcoming.

Economic Activities

Vigorous and widespread economic activities can unquestionably lead to some acceptance of national politics, national policies, national goals and possibly to legitimacy of a unitary national government.

For Uganda the years 1945 to 1962 are best described as years of general economic retardation.

By 1917 Uganda and Kenya had a common market arrangement designed to guarantee free movement of goods between the two British territories and set up a wall against imports unauthorized by the colonial officials. The common market arrangement did not in any way benefit the Africans until the end of World War II, since the two territories were producers of primary commodities for the needs of European markets.

After 1945 colonial policy tried to make Kenya a white man's country through schemes that made economic opportunities attractive enough to allure unemployed whites in Europe to migrate and settle in Kenya. Large fertile tracts of land and cheap labor were made available for Europeans. The East African industrial licensing board provided safeguards for settlers' investments in Kenya for the East African market. Clearly, colonial design during 1945-55 was to make white-controlled Nairobi and the surrounding area the political, commercial and industrial capital of East Africa.

What this colonial economic design meant for Uganda was that Uganda was to remain primarily a producer of coffee, tea, cotton and some cheap textiles, while importing large quantities of agricultural products from the white settlers in Kenya.

As late as 1965 Uganda was importing large quantities of meat, meat preparations, milk products, unmilled wheat, meal and wheat flour, biscuits, onions, animal feed, shortening, vegetable oil, paints, soaps, cleansing materials, insecticides, disinfectants, paper products, blankets of all materials, foot wear, etc. Notably, these articles were the kind that could have been economically produced in Uganda. Consequently, by the end of 1970, Uganda's paid work-force was no more than 300,000 out of a population of ten million. To rectify the economic situation inherited from colonial rule, Dr. Obote's government dared to create economic development programs aimed at doubling per capita income of the peoples of Uganda by 1981--an undertaking that required domestic production in the monetary sector of a growth rate of gross domestic product approximating 8.4 per cent per year.

In order to realize the target rate of growth, the government undertook considerable investment in the construction and building material production. Between 1964 and 1971, government investments in construction had increased 4 times and was expected to increase 13 times by 1981. The investment resulted in most building materials being produced in Uganda, and a considerable increase in the import of machinery and equipment--the kind of goods that were not being produced and unlikely to be produced within the East African common market in the near future. Rapid expansion of the construction industry was necessary and urgently needed for two main reasons:

1. To provide locally produced construction and building materials needed for building other domestic industries and for the construction of roads.

2. To provide locally produced materials for the rapid increase in housing construction activities and general development of urban environment for the ever increasing proportion of Africans living in large towns and cities.

The imediate need for market expansion in imports of equipment and machinery for the construction, building and other industries made it necessary for Uganda not only to restrain the import of other items but also to implement an accelerated program of import substitution so as to keep within the foreign exchange constraint. Import substitution took place mainly in the areas of agricultural products, processed foods, etc., the goods that Uganda could easily produce to supply the local markets, thereby releasing foreign exchange for capital goods. By the end of 1970 Uganda had substituted 25 per cent of the food products originally imported from Kenya with their own products.

Immediately after independence Dr. Obote's government undertook the task of boosting animal husbandry, animal production and milk production in Uganda. Opening a fifteen million dollar milk processing plant of 135,000 litres (30,000 gallons) minimum milk capacity per day in Kampala in November, 1970, the vice president and minister of animal industry, game

and fisheries, Mr. J. K. Bakika, described
the plant as a symbol of Uganda's undisput-
able victories in the area of animal industry. The plant has facilities for making
butter, fresh cream, ice cream, and ghee.
According to Mr. Bakika, the plant was
going to process large quantities of milk
to meet all the country's liquid milk re-
quirements.[15] It is remarkable that through
modern ranching schemes and government milk
cooling processing, programs in cattle
grazing areas has almost tripled milk production in the country in a matter of eight
years. The government efforts in this area
are highly commendable when one realizes
that successful import substitution of
milk, meat, cream, butter, ghee and cheese
alone, mean total savings of $8,500,000 in
Uganda's foreign exchange. It also means
a sizeable increase of Uganda's gross domestic product.

Other vigorous economic activities
have also led to considerable economic
growth in most sectors of the economy (including power, transportation and manufac-
turing). Through these activities as
prescribed by the 1966-71 development
plan, the government hoped to double the
country's 1968 annual per capita income by
1981. The 1966-71 development plan encom-
passed expansion of hotels and the building
of new hotels and lodges to boost the
tourist trade. On the industrial front was
a $15,736,000 investment for extensions to
the fertilizer factor at Tororo designed to
increase the supply of triple superphosphate
to meet the growing East African demands.

Among the major projects planned was
to participate in a multi-million pound in-
tegrated iron and steel project at Tororo,

where locally available magnetite could be used for production of finished steel products (for which there are great demands throughout East Africa). By 1963 the factory at Jinja came into production with an annual production capacity of 25,000 tons of steel, smelted from locally collected iron ore. In July, 1967, a steel tube mill was completed in Jinja for production of electric conduct tubing and steel furniture tubins, as well as tubing for building and general industrial purposes. By the end of 1968 expectations were high that soon bolts, nuts, steel rivets, nails and similar articles would be locally produced for local needs and export within Africa.

The most realistic and impressive project on the heavy industrial scene was the spinning mill in Lira. Uganda was going to change her role as an exporter of vast amounts of raw cotton into a major supplier of yarns. Construction of the plant began in early 1969, involving an investment of $11,802,000 with a loan in equipment from Russia. According to the *Reporter*, the double twisted cotton yarn would be able to utilize 4,500 tons of raw cotton a year, earning Uganda an export revenue of $7,025,000 yearly. Other projects included a $1,405,000 tannery at Soroti in Eastern Uganda to semi-process skins for export and a $2,810,000 salt project at Lake Katwe where natural salt brine was abundant and capable of meeting all salt needs for domestic consumption and for utilization in chemicals. Since colonization, Uganda has imported most of its salt. A fish cannery and dehydrating vegetable factory were among the new projects expected to create export markets. By early 1970, plans for production of rice and soya beans for processing oils, were being studied. High quality printed textile production at Nyanza Textile Industries was also being planned.

In short, Uganda has been having an industrial escalation that would eventually move the society into a new material culture. The high electric power potential and assistance from abroad made it possible for Obote's government to establish and maintain continued economic growth in industry and agriculture. The Owen Falls Hydro-Electric scheme alone produced 574,476,806 units, including 199,112,700 units exported to Kenya from January to November, 1969. Given the great electric power potential and the discoveries of various minerals in the country, the government found itself confident and optimistic that Uganda was at an "industrial take-off" by the beginning of her seventh year as an independent state. Expectations were heightened in July, 1970, when the minister of mineral and water resources, Mr. M. L. Chandry, told Parliament in Kampala that, "Rich deposits of very high quality vermiculite, magnetite, iron, columbite, tantalite, salt and tin had been discovered in different parts of Uganda. Copper, diamonds and wolfram were also being suspected in parts of Karimoja."[16]

The prospects of rapid economic growth were promising. The achievements so far were remarkable according to the annual report of the Bank of Uganda.[17] The value of Uganda's overseas export in 1969 (custom date) of $198,372,000 was an all time record for the country's trade performance, showing an increase of 6.7 per cent over the $186,429,000 worth of goods exported to overseas destinations in 1968. Consequently, Uganda had a favorable overseas trade balance of $70,503,000 in 1969 which was $7,180,000 higher than that of 1968. The overseas imports showed a decline of 8.3 per cent. The report stated that Uganda's gross domestic products (GDP) at factory cost and at prevailing prices grew by 12.5 per cent between 1968 and 1969, and development expenditures at a level of $62,593,000 in 1969-70 were 8 per cent higher than 1968-69. Coffee export earnings registered a rise of 9.1 per cent. Copper exports rose by 7.8 per cent, while that of tea showed an increase of 25.3 per cent. Such economic escalations and successes can be attributed to some government participation and centralized government planning.

In spite of remarkable economic achievements since independence, most peasants have remained outside the new economic activities and benefits. The peasantry remained unhappy with the national government and Obote because the coffee and cotton prices have been on a steady decline since independence. Coffee prices reached their peak in 1955 when the price paid to primary producers by processors was 21 cents per pound. In the early sixties the price was 11 to 13 cents per pound. In September, 1968, coffee prices ranged between 4 to 6 cents per pound. Coffee and cotton are the main source of income for most Ugandans. In Buganda these two products are the main source of income for over 95 per cent of the people.

It was very unfortunate that the national government could do very little, if anything, to alleviate this situation. Not much could be done because in 1964 the

International Coffee Organization and the
International Cotton Organization fully established themselves as the central forum
for international coffee and cotton prices
and policies. For instance, the agreement
proposed by the International Coffee Council in London allocated Uganda a maximum
export quota of 134,000 tons for 1968-69.
It was about the same as in 1967-68. But
the coffee crop of 1968-69 was estimated to
be as high as 230,000 tons. The Uganda
government, like the other underdeveloped
agricultural countries, was caught in a
situation where they had to overship their
agricultural products at the expense of
relatively more favorable international
prices. Since it was politically undesirable to order the peasantry to cut down
their only source of income, coffee and
cotton trees, it was likely that the international coffee and cotton markets would
continue to be swamped with coffee and
cotton--hence driving the prices lower and
lower.

   The peasantry was neither aware nor
capable of understanding the economic
world. What they knew was that prices were
fixed by Obote's government. They also
knew from newspaper and presidential
speeches that 100 per cent of the U. S.
exports to Uganda, amounting to more than
$5,620,000 in 1966, were paid for with
dollars earned from sales of coffee to the
U.S. Since coffee and cotton constitute
more than 60 per cent of Uganda's foreign
exchange earnings, the farmers came to view
Obote as corrupt and responsible for the
low coffee and cotton prices. In Buganda,
the small farmers (who constitute more than
2 million people) associate low prices with
new hotel and lodge development schemes,

with milk machines and other projects of industrialization. They knew that milk coolers were bought with money earned through coffee and cotton sales. To the small farmers Obote and his government took money away from them and gave it to his brothers in northern Uganda who happen to be cattle grazers.

The new hotels and lodges were aspects of modernization that are completely removed from the peasantry. Uganda has preserved her great and wonderful natural heritage--wildlife. Since independence the field of tourism has been booming at a good rate of foreign exchange. Hotels and lodges are built either in Kampala or in places near the wildlife, places removed from the peasantry. To the peasantry their money is being spent on projects of unwarranted unprofitable luxury. In the eyes of most small farmers Obote has been unfair, corrupt, a shameless brute and an economic exploiter. The peasantry believes that a large portion of their hard-earned money from coffee, cotton, tea and tobacco crops was retained by the central government and used for buying machinery, building materials, Mercedes Benzes, guns, jets and comfortable carts for the Uganda army and air force and for Dr. Obote's personal army --the secret police. These expenditures, as far as the peasantry was concerned, were of material and prestigious benefits for Dr. Obote, his friends and his government.

What the peasants believed may not necessarily have been true, but what appeared to them as the truth was bound to play a decisive role in determining whether Dr. Obote was able or unable to generate support for himself and for the government.

In addition to the small coffee, cotton, tea and tobacco farmers were those whose economic activities and well being were inevitably affected by low cash crop prices. The economic prosperity of the small farmers also meant economic prosperity for thousands of small businessmen throughout Uganda. Those who raise cattle, goats and chickens found their incomes much better when the small farmers had money to spend. In a sense Uganda's internal economic activities depended heavily on the money that cash crops could receive from the international market.

The masses as a whole had either directly or indirectly felt the impact of the unfortunate decline of coffee and cotton prices. For instance, government sources claim that medical services have been more than tripled since independence. New hospitals and new dispensaries have been built and opened in different districts of the country. In the meantime, however, the population has grown from 6 million (1959 census) to 9 million by the 1969 census. Most important is the fact that more and more of the peasantry have come to accept modern medical services. At the same time the peasantry found itself economically unable to receive medical help from private doctors and privately owned medical centers. When coffee and cotton prices were high, thousands of the peasants had enough money to afford visits to self-employed doctors and privately owned medical centers. Since independence, more and more peasants have found themselves with no choice but to go to government medical centers dispensing free medicine and medical services.

The medical problems of Uganda are best appreciated when one realizes that in most parts of Uganda there are as many as 25,000 people per medical doctor. In the United States where estimates show 740 people for every medical doctor, there is talk of a shortage of medical doctors and personnel. Uganda, being a society of relatively poor people whose hygienic knowledge is inadequate, needs many more medical personnel and facilities. It is therefore no surprise that in Uganda thousands of people congregate at government medical centers each day. To some patients it means waiting for 3 to 5 hours at the hospital, dispensary or maternity hospitals before they can have a 3 to 10 minute interview with a medical assistant or doctor. Dr. Obote and his government may have done all they could, given the resources available. But as far as the masses were concerned, medical services were far from adequate. The ever-increasing demand for modern medical services in the country, the low income of most small farmers, and the rise in population were bound to shadow the central government's all-out effort to improve the health of the peoples of Uganda.

Given the political history of Uganda, the circumstances under which Obote consolidated his political power and the inherent problems and contradictions of the process of modernization, one can make a few relatively reliable generalizations.

Dr. Obote made himself a giant statesman in the history of Uganda when he dared and successfully eradicated traditional authority in Uganda and put the country on the road to dynamic genuine long run economic, political and social benefit for all Ugandans. Nevertheless, he was never in position (nor was there hope that he would ever be in position) to give the people of Uganda an identity, a common sense of direction, purpose and destiny that would have enabled him to transform his dictatorship into a democratic representative government. Dr. Obote was bound to remain in the eyes of most Ugandans, a ruthless, cold, morally corrupt power grabber. All possibilities considered, Obote was destined to hold power for as long as the police and the army were prepared to enforce his authority.

Conclusion

The purpose of this study was neither to question, to criticize nor to excuse anyone's political actions before or after independence nor to search for solutions for Uganda's numerous political, social and economic problems. It has been an attempt to make an objective diagnosis of Uganda's political environment in order to understand why relatively ruthless authoritarian rule in Uganda came to be not only a necessary but an inevitable stage of Uganda's political development.

Conclusion ; 165

Professor David Truman, like many other political scientists, suggests that a leader has two primary responsibilities--first, to continue himself in office and second, to keep the group together. Dr. Obote was no exception to this general rule. Unfortunately, the conditions under which he had grabbed, monopolized and forcibly retained political power were such that the more determined he was to do both, the more resentment and opposition he created for himself. Almost every step that Obote took to consolidate his own position and national unity appear to have made more personal and political enemies than friends. Dr. Obote's admirable ability and determination to establish his authority in all parts of the country led to government policies that unfortunately made a large majority of Ugandans believe that he was creating a government of the privileged few, by the privileged few and for the privileged few who were willing to be subservient to Dr. Obote's personal aspirations.

The gold and ivory charges were in themselves a blow to Obote's political position. Obote's reaction, in ordering the arrest of five cabinet ministers, including Mr. Grace Ibingira, made matters worse. Mr. Ibingira was a very influential member of Parliament from West Ankole, minister of state and secretary general of the UPC, at the time of his arrest. Writing in 1968, a Uganda citizen from West Ankole expressed what appeared to be the feeling of most people. "Those of us who still believed in him, thought that soon trials would begin and his innocence would free him. Still some of us thought that if he was found guilty of committing treason, then we would elect a new member in a by-election."[1]

The supporters and the sympathizers of Mr. Ibingira and the other ministers within and outside the UPC and the government were appalled by the fact that such important people could be arrested and detained for years without trial.

The cabinet ministers were arrested on February 22, 1966. On February 24, Obote suspended the 1962 constitution, dissolved the Uganda Parliament and declared the office of president and vice president abolished. Neither the members of Parliament nor the people they represented were happy about the drastic changes that they could not understand. Obote seemed to be going on his own at the expense of all vested interests in the name of "national unity," a concept that meant very little if anything to most peoples of Uganda.

Adding fuel to the fire, Obote declared a state of emergency for all Uganda on May 22, 1966, and declared himself president, vice president and prime minister of Uganda. He imposed his own constitution which instantly transformed Uganda from a federal and semi-federal system into a unitary state, abolishing all local governments. At this point Obote had begun to lose many of his sympathizers and supporters who understood his problems but feared the possibilities of a one-man dictatorship.

The military victory of Obote over the Kabaka of Buganda and the new constitution which abolished the four kingdoms in favor of a unitary state made Obote's victory over traditional structures of power unquestionable. Obote's victory, however was a guarantee that he would never be a popular political leader in Buganda, Ankole, Toro, Bunyoro and Busoga Kingdoms. Even the people of Bugangazzi and Buyanda who had reason to see Obote, who had freed them from Buganda Kingdom, as a just and fair leader found themselves viewing Obote as an enemy. They had voted to return to Bunyoro Kingdom jurisdiction only to find themselves peoples without a king.

Most important, it seems, was the inevitable fact that, with the traditional leaders out of sight, the peasants were suddenly to discover that political and economic power was no longer in their respective ethnic capitals but in a government removed physically and emotionally from the rural people. The naked truth was that political and economic power had drastically shifted from the traditional ways and values to urban elites. It was Obote's government, foreign and illegitimate, as far as the peasants were concerned, that was to monopolize the allocation of national resources and directly try to change the peasants' life styles through centrally designed economic development and the national service programs. Given the nature of small scale peasant farming, it was apparent that unless an immediate rise in farm productivity and a sudden improvement in the standard of living in rural areas took place, Obote would never win the hearts of the masses. *The Common Man's Charter* was Dr. Obote's most impressive policy statement on making Uganda a common man's country.

However, it was all too apparent that while the masses were the central focus of Obote's expressed desires for the betterment of Uganda, most resources were in fact devoted to the demands of Dr. Obote's elites and government political clientele. While the government was in position to spend considerable sums of money for the police, army, air force, new TV stations, radio stations and particularly on the general service unity or "secret police," the government was neither in position to provide free fertilizers for the small farmers nor free education for the children of most peasants for whom educational expenses were beyond their means.

While the government was proposing to put all means of production in the hands of the people ("move to the Left" declared by Dr. Obote in late 1969), the people found themselves not only with little direct economic benefits in terms of wages and salaries but also threatened with legal actions if they ever wanted to strike as a means of pushing for better wages. In short, the more Obote concentrated power, the more grievances the people directed against Obote and his government.

Sensitive to the fact that his popularity was diminishing with time, Obote became less and less tolerant of criticisms and political activities of his actual and potential political opponents. The Preventive Detention Act and the state of emergency in Buganda were soon to become Obote's political guillotine.

Those who dared call upon the government to take matters of the five ex-ministers and other political prisoners to the high court were intimidated with arrest, labelled stooges of foreign interests or imprisoned. Abubaker Kakyama Mayanja, Cambridge educated lawyer, ex-minister of education in Buganda government and close associate of Dr. Obote and UPC member of Parliament from Buganda, took issue in writing with government policy that called for a judiciary that takes ideological considerations into account when deciding a case. Mr. Mayanja, in his letter published in the thirty-seventh issue of *Transition*, argued against a judiciary with ideological commitment and accused the government of prolonging the use of what he called outmoded colonial laws, especially those designed by the British to curtail freedom of association and expression. He also accused Dr. Obote's government of dragging its feet on Africanization of the Uganda High Court.

On October 18, soon after Mr. Mayanja's letter was published, Mr. Mayanja and Mr. Rajat Neogy, the editor of *Transition*, were arrested and detained under emergency regulations in Buganda.

Under emergency regulations the person detained had to be apprised of the charges against him, but the government was under no obligation to bring those detained to trial or to make public the charges on which they were detained. Sir William Wilberforce Nadiope, former king of Busoga, former vice president of Uganda and a man with an apparently large following in Busoga, was also detained without trial. Mr. Sebukima, a Makerere University political science student, was also arrested for writing an anonymous letter criticizing the new Uganda constitution. Mr. John Okello (field marshall of 1964 Zanzibar Revolution), was arrested and detained in December, 1966, for the speech he made in Lango District, in which he declared his intentions for starting a Peoples' Socialist party whose goals were national unity, to fight black colonialism, black capitalism and nepotism.

In less than two and one-half years after the 1966 crisis there were more than 50 important political prisoners. By the middle of 1969, it was apparent that Obote's patience with political opponents was irreversibly wearing out. Sir Wilberforce Nadiope stated on March 7, 1971, in Kampala that more than 4,000 people had been held in detention during the nine years Dr. Obote was in power compared with only 35 people detained during the 70 years of British colonial rule.[2] It was very unlikely that in the political intimidations and imprisonments Dr. Obote found the political security he needed. It was apparent that the larger the number of political detainees, less were the chances of dialogue between Dr. Obote and various organized and unorganized intellectual groups. By the middle of 1969, a climate of distrust, suspicion, fear and hate of Dr. Obote's authority was taking over the country.

The assassination attempt on Obote's life on December 19, 1969, plunged Uganda deeper into ruthless authoritarian rule. Dr. Obote was fired at as he was leaving the UPC delegation conference in Kampala. Following the assassination attempt, the state of emergency which had been in force in Buganda since May, 1966, was extended to the whole country. Dr. Obote became super sensitive to his dwindling public support and fearful for his life; he therefore used the opportunity to ban all opposition organizations and membership societies. The Democratic party, the Uganda National Union, Uganda Farmers Voice and Uganda National Socialist party were among the groups banned. On December 20, 1969, Mr. Benedict Kiwanuka, a lawyer, first prime minister of Uganda and president of the Democratic party (the only opposition party in Parliament), was arrested and detained. Mr. Paul Ssemogerere, publicity secretary of the Democratic party who had since early 1967 persistantly called upon Dr. Obote's government to allow political activities and to provide free and fair elections, was also arrested and detained. The assassination attempt marked the beginning of actual and effective one party politics in Uganda.

By the end of 1969, it was apparent that Obote's political problems were not only with the masses who had viewed his government since 1966 as nothing short of tyranny and illegitimate dictatorship, but also with the intellectuals and semi-educated who had earlier been sympathetic to Obote's bid for national unity but never envisioned the possibility of a one party state, based on a high degree of Obote's necessary disregard for human rights and democratic principles.

As if to answer his critics abroad and to save face with the neighboring heads of state in Congo Kinshasha, Tanzania and Kenya, Dr. Obote declared in early 1970 that general elections would be held in April, 1971. The hopes and high expectations emanating from the possibility of a fair and free election plunged Obote into further isolation from the people. In August, 1970, Dr. Obote's party's delegates conference, meeting at Mbale, passed a resolution which made the ruling party's leader automatically the country's president. The resolution provoked immediate negative reactions from all quarters, including Dr. Obote's friends and sympathizers in and outside the party. The overwhelming majority of Ugandans were calling for a president elected by all the people and not by a few individuals who happened to be invited as delegates to the conference.

In any case, it did not matter how the president was to be elected, for the elections were to take place in April, 1971, while the former Buganda Kingdom (including Kampala, the political, economic, educational and communication center of Uganda) was still under the state of emergency declared in May, 1966. However, all potential and actual competent contestants for the presidency were in prison under emergency regulations. In theory and in fact, Obote had wrapped up the entire political situation to insure his re-election, unopposed, for the next five years. In addition, only UPC candidates would run for office, and all parliamentary candidates were to be selected by a new body called the presidential commission. The commission owed its existence and legitimacy to Obote personally. Dr. Obote appointed all commissioners who would in turn pick three candidates for each of the 96 parliamentary constituencies.

The results of the pending elections were definitely pre-ordained, anguishing most citizens at the prospects of Dr. Obote rule for the next five years. It was apparent that the proposed general elections were to be a mere tool for Dr. Obote to eliminate anti-Obote and anti-socialism elements in Parliament and to establish a national Parliament of his hand-picked men through the presidential commission. Dr. Obote further tightened his grip on the country by proposing that the president would nominate his own interim successor, whose name would be in a sealed envelope to be opened only in the event of the president's death, resignation or removal. The name was to be a High Court judge.

Dr. Obote's plots and purposes were clear. He wanted to by-pass the vice president and all members of Parliament and all possible candidates. Obote was to appoint the high court judges, and from them he would choose his interim successor. It was already becoming common gossip in Uganda that Akena Adoka, Obote's cousin and head of the "secret police" or the general service department, was to be Obote's first choice for the high court. Mr. Akena, a lawyer who had never practiced law but had become president of Uganda Law Society by government policy, was destined to be the high court judge in the sealed envelope. Mr. Akena was not only the most feared man (as head of the secret police and the most powerful man in the country after President Obote) but also believed to have been the author or co-author of the Common Man's Charter and the *Nakivubo Pronouncement*, which officially put Uganda on a socialist path.

Step by step, Dr. Obote had not only consolidated his positions but also had made changes and placed Uganda on a path that seemed impossible to change through democratic means. By the end of 1970, the people were certain that Dr. Obote would not leave the state house in any foreseeable future unless by physical elimination or by forcible overthrow carried out by the only powerful, highly organized and disciplined group within Uganda--the military.

Out of Dr. Obote's ruthless dictatorship there was the hope that the peoples of Uganda would be roused to a new social and political consciousness. In time Obote would have become the only national symbol as the object of fear, hate and resentment. In other words, in Dr. Obote's ruthlessness lay his main significant contribution toward national consciousness. Out of oppression most Ugandans were bound to see politics in a new light. Under Obote political life was bound to become more and more significant in terms of political alternatives other than ethnic group politics. For the masses lay the opportunities for a widespread dynamic awareness of the possibilities of political, social and economic changes and progress. Out of Obote's ruthless authoritarian rule a new republic of Uganda, based on a new kind of social, economic and political consciousness, was bound to emerge.

Dr. Obote's days as despotic manager and owner of Uganda came to an abrupt end on January 25, 1971. Dr. Obote's hand picked military leaders suppressed his plans and relieved him of an impossible task of containing Uganda for the next five to ten years.

It is too early to say confidently where Uganda will go after the relatively bloodless military overthrow of Dr. Obote. But a number of things are clear. The day of Dr. Obote's complete and apparently permanent downfall was not only the day of freedom for the political prisoners immediately released by the military government but also a day of freedom and intense jubilation for a very large majority of the peoples of Uganda.

Upon the announcement that the Uganda Armed Forces had seized control of Obote's government, there was nationwide instantaneous public jubilation. According to Uganda's newspapers and letters from my brother and friends, large crowds gathered, cheered, tore Dr. Obote's pictures off private and public places and danced in the streets. It is unquestionable that in most parts of Uganda the public reacted with great joy and excitement. As Major General Idi Amin Dada, the head of Uganda's military government, put it, "A great heavy weight had been lifted off the shoulders of the general public and so they went almost wild with joy."[3]

Most encouraging was the immediate willingness of the peasants, civil servants, workers, industrial agencies, students and intellectuals to cooperate with the military government. The military government also promised to return Ugandan politics to civilians through a free and fair general election. General Amin is the first national image Uganda has ever had and a person other than a king, prince or traditional leader that the masses from all parts of Uganda have been able to regard as a legitimate authoritative leader. /General Amin has emerged as a national symbol of / unity, peace and social justice.

If the military government is well advised to uphold the republican principles and a unitary government introduced and implemented by Dr. Milton Obote since 1966, Uganda may well be finished with the possibilities and inevitabilities of authoritarian rule. The new political consciousness can serve as a basis for a new republic whose politics will be determined by factors other than traditionalists vs. nationalists. It is now feasible to have a central government with widespread and genuine popular support, or at least acquiescence, from each and every corner of Uganda.

As a Muganda, a political science student and a politically sensitive and concerned citizen of Uganda, I have no doubt that Uganda's political life and environment after the coup are better than ever before for a true democratic and representative political system.

Notes

INTRODUCTION

1. David E. Apter, "September, 1960 Memorandum to Her Majesty Queen Elizabeth II," *The Political Kingdom in Uganda* (Princeton, New Jersey: Princeton Univ. Press, 1961), pp. 479-488.

2. Apolo Msitami, "Political Integration in Uganda: Problems and Prospects," *East African Journal*, February 1969, p. 31.

NOTES - Introduction : 177

3. Charles R. Adrian and Charles Press, *Governing Urban American*, 3rd ed. (New York: McGraw Hill, 1968), p. 71.

4. C. E. Black, *The Dynamics of Modernization* (New York: Harper & Row, 1966), p. 65.

5. *Transition Magazine* (Kampala, Uganda), October 18, 1968, p. 10.

CHAPTER 1

1. *London Times*, October 9, 1962, p. viii.

2. Kiswahili (French Language of East Africa).

3. John A. Hobson, "Imperialism: The Classic Statement," *British Imperialism*, ed. Robin W. Winks (New York: Holt, Rinehart & Winston, 1963), p. 12.

4. *Ibid.*, p. 12.

5. Ronald Cohen, "Traditional Society in Africa," *The African Experience*, vol. I, ed. Paden and Soja (Evanston, Illinois: Northwestern Univ. Press, 1970), p. 60.

6. Eduardo Chimamko Mondlane; born 1920, Mozambique;educated Lamania Secondary School South Africa, Oberlin College Ohio U.S.A., Northwestern University B.A., M.A., Ph.D.; Research Officer, Trusteeship Department United Nations, 1947-61; Lecturer in Anthropology, Syracuse University, 1961-63; President, Mozambique Liberation Front until his assassination late 1968.

7. Fred G. Burke, "Unity and Diversity in East Africa . . . A synthesisless Dialectic," an address prepared for an delivered at Duke University's Commonwealth Studies Center, February 15, 1965.

8. David B. Truman, *The Governmental Process* (New York: Alfred A. Knopf, 1967), p. 4.

9. *Ibid.*, p. 4.

10. Bantu is a linguistic grouping of black Africans which includes the Basoga, Baganda, Banyoro, Batoro, Banyankole and Bachiga in Uganda.

11. May M. Edel, *The Chiga of Western Uganda* (New York: Oxford Univ. Press, 1957), p. 2.

12. *Ibid.*, p. 3.

13. *Ibid.*, p. 23.

14. *Ibid.*, p. 112.

15. *Ibid.*, p. 113.

16. *London Times*, October 9, 1962, p. ix.

17. Neville Dyson-Hudson, *Karamojong Politics* (Oxford: Clarendon Press, 1966), p. 211.

18. *Ibid.*, p. 115.

19. The initiation ceremony is a religious neighborhood congregation whereby young people are circumcized and officially

NOTES - The Pre-Colonial Period : 179

welcomed into the adult world and made members of a particular age group in Karamojong society.

20. Dyson-Hudson, *Karamojong Politics*, p. 156.

21. *Ibid.*, p. 218.

22. David E. Apter, *The Political Kingdom in Uganda* (Princeton, New Jersey: Princeton Univ. Press, 1961), p. 87.

23. *Ibid.*, p. 96.

24. *Ibid.*, p. 97.

CHAPTER 2

1. Apter, *The Political Kingdom,* p. 66.

2. Sir John Gray, "Sir John Kirk and Mutesa," *Uganda Journal* 1 (March 1951): 1-2.

3. Apter, *The Political Kingdom,* p. 64.

4. Mackay, as quoted in *The Political Kingdom,* p. 65.

5. Kenneth Ingham, Professor of History at Makerere College, The University of East Africa.

6. Kenneth Ingham, *The Making of Modern Uganda* (Ruskin House; George Allen & Unwin, Ltd., 1958), p. 14.

7. "J. H. Speke's Journal of the Discovery of the Source of the Nile," *The Making of Modern Uganda*, p. 14.

8. Ingham, *The Making of Modern Uganda*, p. 35.

9. Apter, *The Political Kingdom*, p. 66.

10. Ronald Robinson, "Anderson's Cabinet Memo," *Africa and the Victorians* (Garden City: Anchor Books, 1968), p. 203.

11. Ronald Robinson, *Africa and the Victorians*, p. 309.

12. William Harcourt, as quoted in *Africa and the Victorians*, p. 315.

13. Lloyd A. Fallers, *The King's Men: Leadership and Status in Buganda on the Eve of Independence* (London: Oxford Univ. Press, 1964), p. 309.

14. Apter, *The Political Kingdom*, p. 77.

15. A. D. Roberts, "The Sub-Imperialism of the Baganda," *The Journal of African History* III, 3 (1962): 435.

16. *Ibid.*, p. 439.

17. *Ibid.*, p. 435.

18. The British-Buganda Agreement of 1900.

19. Roberts, "Sub-Imperialism," p. 438.

NOTES - The Colonial Experience ; 181

20. Ibid., p. 440.

21. Michael Twaddle, "The Bakungu Chiefs of Buganda under British Colonial Rule, 1900-1930," *The Journal of African History* X, 2 (1969): 309-322.

22. Ibid., p. 335.

23. Ibid., p. 447.

24. Figures from *Uganda: The Pearl of Africa*, by the ministry of information, broadcasting and tourism (Kampala: The Uganda Argus, Ltd.), pp. 434-44 and p. 47.

25. J. P. Barber, "The Karamoja District of Uganda, a Pastoral People under Colonial Rule," *The Journal of African History* III, 1 (1962): 111.

26. Ibid., p. 239.

27. Ibid., p. 113.

28. Ibid., p. 115.

29. Ibid., p. 117.

30. Ibid., p. 121.

31. Ibid., p. 237.

32. Nelson Kasfir, "Toro District: Society and Politics," *Mawazo* (Kampala, Uganda: Makerere Univ. Publications), II, 3 (1970): 39. Original statistics from *Uganda Statistical Abstract*, p. 11.

33. Ibid., p. 39.

182 : UGANDA

    34. *Ibid.*, p. 43.

    35. *Ibid.*, p. 45.

CHAPTER 3

    1. Truman, *The Governmental Process*, p. 14.

    2. *Ibid.*, p. 19.

    3. *Ibid.*, p. 511.

    4. *Ibid.*, p. 511.

    5. *Ibid.*, p. 505.

    6. Cycil Ehrlich, *The Marketing of Cotton in Uganda* (University of London Library, 1958).

    7. Twaddle, "The Bakungu Chiefs of Buganda," pp. 309-10.

    8. *Ibid.*

    9. Dr. Joseph Kiwanuka, Archbishop of Rubaga, *Ebbaluwa ya Ssabepiskopi Kiwanuka Okutangaza Abakatoliki Mu By'obufuzi* (Kisubi, Uganda: Marianum Press), XII 61; 10M.

    10. C. J. Gertzel, "New Government in Uganda," *Africa Report* May 1962, p. 8.

    11. D. A. Low, *Political Parties in Uganda, 1949-1962* (University of London: Athlone Press, 1962), pp. 13-14.

12. M. Kintu, "Buganda's Position" (Information Dept., Kabaka's Government, Kampala, Uganda Printing & Publishing Co., 1960), pp. 1-2.

13. Thomas Hodgkin, *African Political Parties* (Baltimore, Maryland: Penguin Books, 1962), p. 138.

14. *The Journal of African History* III, 1 (1962): 236.

15. Dyson-Hudson, *Karamojong Politics*, p. 211.

CHAPTER 4

1. Fallers, *The King's Men*, p. 332.

2. *Ibid.*, p. 322.

3. *Ibid.*, p. 322.

4. *Ibid.*, p. 359.

5. Kabaka Yekka was an ethnic political party organized by traditionalists and neo-traditionalists in Buganda. Kabaka Yekka means "king only" or "king alone." The Kabaka of Buganda, Sir Edward Mutesa II, was head of Kabaka Yekka by implication.

6. A. I. Richards, "Epilogue," *The King's Men* (Oxford Univ. Press, 1964), p. 358.

7. C. J. Gertzel, "Report from Kampala," *Africa Report*, October 1964, p. 12.

8. *Ibid.*, p. 10.

CHAPTER 5

1. Gertzel, "New Government in Uganda," p. 8.

2. *Ibid.*, p. 8.

3. Fallers, *The King's Men*, p. 361.

4. Martin Lowenkopf, "Uganda's Prime Minister Obote," *Africa Report*, October 1962, p. 11.

5. Low, *Political Parties in Uganda*, p. 12.

6. Gertzel, "Report from Kampala," p. 12.

7. *Ibid.*, p. 10.

8. A. K. Mayanja, "What is Kabaka Yekka?" *Africa Report*, May 1962, p. 13.

9. "News in Brief," *Africa Report*, December 1965, p. 31.

10. M. Crawford Young, "The Obote Revolution," *Africa Report*, June 1966, p. 12.

11. *London Times*, October 9, 1962, p. ix.

12. Kintu, "Buganda's Position," pp. 1-2.

NOTES - Post-Independence Politics : 185

13. Young, "The Obote Revolution," p. 8.

14. *Uganda Newsletter* (Uganda Embassy Publication W.D.C.), January 1970.

15. *Ibid.*

CHAPTER 6

1. Demands: Services and policies which individuals, organized groups and potential groups desire from their government.

2. Out-puts: Services and policies government provides as a positive or negative response to the demands of its citizens.

3. Feedback: The relationships between demands and out-puts and the consequences of the relationships.

4. David Easton, Ph.D., Harvard University, is Professor of political science at the University of Chicago and author of *The Political System*.

5. Milton Obote, "Policy Proposal for Uganda's Educational Needs," *Mawazo* (Kampala: Makerere University), II, 2 December, 1969): 3.

6. *Ibid.*, p. 3.

7. *Ibid.*, p. 6.

8. *Ibid.*, p. 4.

9. *Ibid.*, p. 4.

10. L. Gray Cowan, *The Dilemmas of African Independence* (New York: Walker & Co., 1964), p. 114.

11. "News in Brief," *Africa Report,* November 1964, p. 27.

12. "News in Brief," *Africa Report,* October 1964, p. 30.

13. Obote, "Policy Proposal," p. 4.

14. "The Uganda Army: Nexus of Power," *Africa Report,* December 1966, p. 39.

15. J. K. Babika, *Uganda News Letter,* January 1970.

16. M. L. Chandry, *Uganda News Letter,* December 1969.

17. *Ibid.*

CONCLUSION

1. Owawe, "Letter to the Editor," *Reporter,* October 1968, p. 2.

2. *London Times,* March 9, 1971, p. 7.

3. *Uganda Argus* (Kampala), January 28, 1971, p. 1.

Bibliography

Adrian, Charles R. and Press, Charles, *Governing Urban American*. 3rd ed. New York: McGraw Hill, 1968.

Apter, David E. *The Political Kingdom in Uganda*. Princeton, New Jersey: Princeton University Press, 1961.

Babika, J. K. *Uganda News Letter*, January 1970.

Barber, J. P. "The Karamoja District of Uganda, A Pastoral People under Colonial Rule," *The Journal of African History* III, 1 (1962).

Black, C. E. *The Dynamics of Modernization*. New York: Harper and Row, 1966.

Burke, Fred G. "Unity and Diversity in East Africa--A Synthesisless Dialectic." An address given at Duke University's Commonwealth Studies Center, February 15, 1965.

Chandry, M. L. *Uganda News Letter*, December 1969.

Cohen, Ronald. "Traditional Society in Africa." In *The African Experience*, vol. 1, edited by Paden and Soja. Evanston, Illinois: Northwestern University Press, 1970.

Cowan, L. Gray. *The Dilemmas of African Independence*. New York: Walker and Co., 1964.

Dyson-Hudson, Neville. *Karamojong Politics*. Oxford, England: Clarendon Press, 1966.

Edel, May M. *The Chiga of Western Uganda*. New York: Oxford University Press, 1957.

Ehrlich, Cycil. *The Marketing of Cotton in Uganda*. University of London Library, 1958.

Fallers, Lloyd A. *The King's Men: Leadership and Status in Buganda on the Eve of Independence*. London: Oxford University Press, 1964.

Gertzel, C. J. "New Government in Uganda," *Africa Report*, October 1962.

_____. "Report from Kampala," *Africa Report*, October 1964.

Gray, John. "Sir John Kirk and Mutesa," *Uganda Journal* XV, no. 1 (March 1951).

Hobson, John A. "Imperialism: The Classic Statement." In *British Imperialism*, edited by Robin W. Winks. New York: Holt, Rinehart and Winston, 1963.

Hodgkin, Thomas. *African Political Parties*. Baltimore, Maryland: Penguin Books, 1962.

Ingham, Kenneth. *The Making of Modern Uganda*. Ruskin House: George Allen and Unwin, Ltd., 1958.

Kasfir, Nelson. "Toro District: Society and Politics," *Mawazo* II, no. 3. Kampala, Uganda: Makerere University Publications, 1970.

Kintu, M. "Buganda's Position." Information Department, Kabaka's Government, Kampala, Uganda: Uganda Printing and Publishing Co., 1960.

Kiwanuka, Joseph. *Ebbaluwa ya Ssabepiskopi Kiwanuka Okutangaza Abakatoliki mu By'obufuzi.* Kisubi, Uganda: Marianum Press, 1961.

London Times, October 9, 1962.

Low, D. A. *Political Parties in Uganda: 1949-1962.* London: Athlone Press, 1962.

Lowenkopf, Martin. "Uganda's Prime Minister Obote," *Africa Report*, October 1962.

Mayanja, A. K. "What is Kabaka Yekka?" *Africa Report*, May 1962.

Msibambi, Apolo. "Political Integration in Uganda: Problems and Prospects," *East African Journal*, February 1969.

"News in Brief," *Africa Report*, October 1964.

"News in Brief," *Africa Report*, November 1964.

"News in Brief," *Africa Report*, December 1965.

Obote, Milton. "Policy Proposal for Uganda's Educational Needs," *Mawazo* II, no. 2. Kampala, Uganda: Makerere University Publications, 1969.

Reporter, October 1968.

Richard, A. U. Epilogue to *The King's Men: Leadership and Status in Buganda on the Eve of Independence* by Lloyd A. Fallers. London: Oxford University Press, 1964.

Roberts, A. D. "The Sub-Imperialism of the Buganda," *The Journal of African History* III, no. 3 (1962).

Robinson, Ronald. *Africa and the Victorians*. Camden, New Jersey: Anchor Books, 1968.

Transition Magazine, October 18, 1968, p. 10.

Truman, David B. *The Governmental Process*. New York: Alfred A. Knopf, 1967.

Twaddle, Michael. "The Bakungu Chiefs of Buganda under British Colonial Rule, 1900-1930," *The Journal of African History* X, no. 2 (1969), pp. 309-322.

Uganda Argus, January 28, 1971, p. 1.

"The Uganda Army: Nexus of Power," *Africa Report*, December 1966.

Young, M. Crawford. "The Obote Revolution," *Africa Report*, June 1966.